T0320053

Struggle in a Time of Crisis

Struggle in a Time of Crisis

Edited by
Nicolas Pons-Vignon
and Mbuso Nkosi

PlutoPress
www.plutobooks.com

First published 2015 by Pluto Press
345 Archway Road, London N6 5AA

www.plutobooks.com

British Library Cataloguing in Publication Data
A catalogue record for this book is available from the British Library

ISBN   978 0 7453 3616 9   Hardback
ISBN   978 0 7453 3621 3   Paperback
ISBN   978 1 7837 1731 6   PDF eBook
ISBN   978 1 7837 1733 0   Kindle eBook
ISBN   978 1 7837 1732 3   EPUB eBook

This book is printed on paper suitable for recycling and made from fully managed and sustained forest sources. Logging, pulping and manufacturing processes are expected to conform to the environmental standards of the country of origin.

10   9   8   7   6   5   4   3   2   1

Typeset by Stanford DTP Services, Northampton, England
Text design by Melanie Patrick
Simultaneously printed by CPI Antony Rowe, Chippenham, UK
and Edwards Bros in the United States of America

Dedicated to the memory of Frederic Sterling Lee

Contents

List of Figures

Acknowledgements

Earlier versions of the articles in this book were first published in the Global Labour Column (GLC) – http://column.global-labour-university.org/ – which is edited at the University of the Witwatersrand in Johannesburg. The GLC is a project of the Global Labour University, a network of trade unions, universities and the ILO (International Labour Organisation). It offers Masters Courses in five different countries on trade unions, sustainable development, social justice, international labour standards, multinational companies, economic policies and global institutions and promotes research cooperation on global labour issues. The GLU is a new approach to increase the intellectual and strategic capacity of workers' organisations and to establish stronger working relationships between trade unions, the ILO and the scientific community.

We thank the Bureau for Workers' Activities of the ILO for its financial support.

GLOBAL LABOUR
UNIVERSITY

Introduction[1]

Nicolas Pons-Vignon and Mbuso Nkosi

The history of all hitherto existing society is the history of class struggles.

Marx and Engels, *The Communist Manifesto*

The crisis which started in the United States in 2007 has turned into a global depression whose consequences are wreaking havoc across the world, although affecting in a disproportionate manner the 99 per cent, people who depend on their labour or state transfers to live. While banks and large companies have been bailed out (a remarkable sign that state intervention is alive and well in the neoliberal era) it is the majority who are now paying the bill in the form of spending cuts. Such cuts have direct social and economic effects: on the one hand, they make life more difficult for the poor who depend on grants or free access to essential services; on the other hand, they undermine investment and economic recovery, delaying desperately needed job creation. As shown by David Stuckler and Sanjay Basu (2013) in their work on austerity policies' impact on health, austerity kills, not just growth, but people.

The crisis has shown the limits of the neoliberal model of accumulation and of its theoretical or ideological foundation, the neoclassical belief in the self-regulating ability of 'free' markets. This is nothing new though, as many economists outside of the hegemonic neoclassical tradition had been arguing since the 1980s that neoliberal capitalism does not only increase inequality, but generates disequilibria which threaten the possibility of sustained growth. Such debates, which would have appeared far too radical a few years ago, have now entered the mainstream of the economics profession, as shown by the conference organised in March 2015 by the *New York Review of Books* on 'What's Wrong with the Economy – and with Economics?'.[2]

There is, in Europe and North America, a rampant sense of powerlessness in the face of the crisis. This is because, in spite of the rise of numerous

---

1. We thank Gilad Isaacs for comments on this introduction; the usual disclaimers apply.
2. See www.nybooks.com/blogs/gallery/2015/mar/29/whats-wrong-with-the-economy/.

movements of contestation of neoliberal policies, from Occupy to the *Indignados*, the only cure which politicians are implementing to respond to the ills of neoliberalism entails more of the same. The Syriza-led government in Greece is of course the lone exception, but its very ability to prove the 'There is no alternative' dogma wrong means that it is under intense pressure to jettison its hopes of charting an alternative path. The other alternative, of course, which is steadily rising across Europe, is a far-right populism which is worryingly reminiscent of the 1930s.

There is an important difference between the last period of sustained world crisis in the 1930s and now, in that there are no leaders such as Franklin Delano Roosevelt who are prepared to rein in the market. When this was undertaken during the Great Depression, it laid the foundation for an era of 'shared prosperity' between capital and labour after the Second World War. During this so-called Golden Age, wage increases and extensions allowed, in advanced capitalist countries, for an unprecedented reduction in inequality. This explains why the memory of, or perhaps nostalgia for, this age makes it an enduring reference point for much of the left and most trade unions.

Three qualifications to the idealised vision of the Golden Age are important. First, this phase of capitalist accumulation, which has been called Fordism, did not emerge only out of the vision of politicians or businessmen, but was the result of the enormous political power (and threat) of the Communist left, who had played a central and painful part in the resistance to fascism. Secondly, whilst inequality declined, it remained stubbornly present; many in the West, and many more outside of it, did not benefit from institutionalised redistribution. It was perhaps a Golden Age for capitalism, but not one for all workers, let alone inhabitants of the world. Thirdly, as shown by Thomas Piketty (2014), this period was an exception; in the long term, capitalist development is associated with the rise of inequality between capital and labour; neoliberalism has entailed a return to this trend.

Where Piketty, and many of the progressive economists who have sought to make sense of the crisis and propose alternatives, fail to convince is on how a reform agenda can actually be implemented. If anything, the response to the crisis has proved that ideas, however important they may be, are not enough to change the world because deeply-entrenched interests have proved incredibly resilient to crisis, struggle and arguments in favour of alternatives. Take the rise of finance, the central 'disequilibrium' associated with the neoliberal era, which has promoted rapid enrichment at the top without supporting real production. Analysts of financialisation[3] have shown the pervasiveness of finance as well as its articulation with political intervention aimed at pushing the penetration of finance into all areas of human life, including housing for low-income groups, tertiary education and medical care. In the debates that followed the global crisis, calls for the re-regulation of finance have become commonplace, if only for the simple purpose of realigning finance with its *raison d'être*, financing real economic activity, yet we have not seen a decline in financial speculation. The ability of these narrow vested interests to trump the common good can be seen for example in the bailing out of banks whose behaviour had been in many cases irresponsible, and in the ongoing central role that tax havens have come to play in the global economy (see Shaxson, 2011; and Strauss in this volume on taxation). Ironically, this intense concentration of wealth violates the purported notion advanced by neoliberalism that, as the rich get wealthier, all will benefit through trickle down.

While neoliberalism advanced, the left was disintegrating as a coherent political force from the 1980s onwards. After the fall of the Berlin Wall, triumphant anti-Communist commentators announced the end of history, effectively the end of struggles around the formation and distribution of surplus. Problems (whether economic, social or political) could be resolved within the liberal democratic form, through the inclusion of new concerns in policy making, mimicking the way markets respond to new needs. The current inability to take forward progressive responses to the crisis is indeed a reflection of the historical and intellectual defeat of the Western left and of trade unions against neoliberalism. Brazil's *Partido dos Trabalhadores* (Workers' Party) has put it in unambiguous terms:

The left in European countries, which has had such an influence on the left worldwide since the 19th century, has not managed to produce an adequate response to the crisis and appears to be capitulating to the forces of neoliberalism.[4]

3. For an excellent repository of articles on this issue, see the site of Research on Money and Finance: www.researchonmoneyandfinance.org/.
4. Quoted in Serge Halimi (2011) 'Where did the left go?', *Le Monde diplomatique*, November (available at: http://mondediplo.com/2011/11/01left).

The so-called moderate left, formerly social-democratic and now social-liberal, has actually played a critical role in ensuring the domination of neoliberalism. Instead of breaking from it when the traditional left came back to power, whether in Germany or Britain (but also in South Africa), it espoused its most important principles with some cosmetic changes – best illustrated by British New Labour's presentation of decentralisation and public–private partnerships as ways of 'empowering citizens'. Breaking with neoliberalism has to entail the founding of a new left project which can confront capitalism, on the ground as well as at the programmatic level, and which refuses to draw on neoliberal premises, for instance the belief in the alleged superiority of private enterprise over socialised provision or production. With growing evidence of financial and technical failure,[5] reviving debates on alternatives to privatisation is therefore crucial; what is the best way to ensure affordable, quality and democratically-controlled services? Such debates would have much to learn from past experiences, whether social-democratic, socialist or anarcho-syndicalist.

The crisis of the left and of its traditional pillar, trade unionism, is profound – leading many across the political spectrum to believe that it is terminal. This crisis has to do, in the West, with the abandonment of the political struggle which had animated it before the Second World War, to focus entirely on economic struggles to improve the situation of workers. This acceptance of contestation framed within a regulated (capitalist) context created a comfort which made the left subsequently unable (or perhaps unwilling) to respond to the formidable onslaught of neoliberalism. The latter took the form, among others, of the restructuring of production and work under the pretext of greater efficiency. The pervasive use of outsourcing arrangements combined with the decline of manufacturing (where trade unionism was traditionally strongest) and swelled the number of service jobs as workers became employees of service providers. The result was an atomised workforce with fewer industrial workers and a steady decline in the representativity and strength of unions, who failed to make significant inroads into organising in private services, even if this is where growing numbers of workers found themselves.

---

5. See for instance Bowman, A. et al. (2013), *The Great Train Robbery: Rail privatisation and after*, Public interest report by CRESC (University of Manchester), available from: www.cresc.ac.uk/.

This phenomenon lies at the heart of the political weakening of the left, and led to a crucial ideological victory: the belief that the world had entered a post-industrial era in which the traditional opposition between capitalists and the working class, captured by the figure, in the West, of the white male, permanently employed and unionised worker was outdated. More broadly, the working class and the strategic importance of the 'point of production' had become irrelevant since productive organisation was carefully managed by capitalists so as to make workplace contestation irrelevant. This was the basis on which the inclusion of part of the left in the neoliberal consensus became possible – the struggle had somehow changed location, although where to exactly has never been clear.

The decline of trade unionism has been welcome by some on the far left too, who emphasised the limitations (and at times reactionary character) of the dominant left, preferring instead to see atomised social movements as a more desirable agent of progressive change (see for instance Hardt and Negri, 2005). It is true that dynamic social movements have emerged and constituted some of the most visible forms of struggle against neoliberalism. It is equally true that the Golden Age model of trade unionism had many flaws, not least how its 'universal' class agenda hid its discriminatory character. Gender, racial and other forms of discriminatory prejudice and practices still shape much of union activity across the world. These certainly go a long way towards explaining the widespread failure to organise casual workers, for the latter are often non-white, and female. Moreover, trade unions have often found it difficult to create alliances with social movements, even when their struggles seemed aligned.

But do these flaws mean that trade unionism is a dead-end for a renewed left project – or that it needs a profound transformation? We firmly believe in the latter, not least because the very decline of unionism and the illusion of the disappearance of the working class are themselves the result of a deliberate – and successful – strategy by neoliberal capitalists. The importance of trade unions, which are rooted at the heart of capitalist accumulation and therefore have the potential to disrupt it and force capital to make compromises, joining forces with social movements who contest neoliberalism from below, was emphasised by Pierre Bourdieu (2000). He argued that neither would be likely to succeed alone in contesting the power of capital under neoliberalism; this is supported by Felicio in this volume, who acknowledges that the challenge of unifying and co-ordinating struggles is paramount yet extremely difficult. Union struggles are indeed often disconnected, not only from social movements but also from one another; the tensions inherent in the (necessary) globalisation of struggles are explored in depth in this volume, inter alia by Munck and Bieler. We can draw inspiration from South Africa with the National Union of Metal Workers of South Africa (NUMSA) breaking away from its alliance with the ruling party, the African National Congress (ANC) to engage with different social movements and build a united front against neoliberalism (see the interview with Karl Cloete in this volume).

Loose networks and atomised actions, however useful they may be, will never solve the collective problems confronting the majority. This is because what determines change is ultimately related to decisions over budgetary allocation, or sovereign choices, and having influence over these matters is absolutely crucial. To take a local victory to the national or international level entails much higher, sometimes systemic stakes; capitalist resistance to a one-off demand may be tempered in order to prevent it broadening, while for labour it is this broadening which matters most. Even programmes that may appear to have been successful at the local level, such as those to improve working conditions in the garment industry in Cambodia, may prove to be a far cry from real progressive change if they are not firmly controlled by workers, their alleged beneficiaries (Arnold in this volume).

If progressive struggles do not succeed in organising themselves to present an alternative, then the alternative will be either business as usual or far-right populism. The latter has the ability to borrow selectively from the language of the left, as the national socialists from yesterday, to appeal to the majority. But like their predecessors, modern day populists remain a key political instrument for capital, to restore order and trust. They will not challenge inequality but instead make contestation even more difficult. We may be preaching to the convinced, for it is unlikely that many readers of this book doubt (even if they may be tempted out of frustration with established politics) that the far right represents a dead end. The question is then whether a progressive alternative can be built.

For this, the need to make sense of the transformations of capitalism since the 1970s and of their implications is paramount. This means that we need theory and analysis – both to understand and to change the world. Valiani in this volume offers a compelling example by unpacking the reasons behind the structural reliance of North American hospitals on foreign nurses. Exploitation of labour in the neoliberal era has transformed but it remains pervasive; this is particularly clear if one looks at the developments in the global South, from the persistence of slave labour in Brazilian agriculture (Carstensen and McGrath in this volume) to the spate of deadly industrial accidents in Bangladesh (Gross in this volume). Articulating theory with practice means 'learning from the past', as emphasised by Lucien van der Walt (2014: 22) in an address to South African social movements:

> [...] the working class, the poor and the peasants of the world have heroic traditions of struggle going back hundreds of years, from centuries of fighting slavery, colonialism, imperialism, capitalism and state oppression. It is from these experiences that we have developed theory and strategy and vision as a way for us to try to understand that long history.

Indeed, not only does production (and the class exploitation which lies at the core of it) still play a critical role in capitalist accumulation, but it also generates much resistance, some atomised or 'hidden', some very overt and organised. The democratisation of South Korea, Brazil and South Africa in the late twentieth century has been driven by the activism of industrial workers and of their radical unions.

With this book, and the online *Global Labour Column* (GLC) from which the chapters are drawn, we hope to show that labour is not dead as an agent of progressive change, and that many workers and unionists across the world acknowledge the limitations which have hampered their actions before and are keen to build meaningful alliances with other progressive forces. Much of this activism comes from the global South, which is unsurprising given that is where a growing proportion of capitalist production is now taking place and the radical struggles which the painful experience of colonial and post-colonial exploitation gave rise to. We also examine innovative attempts at responding to the damages of globalisation, for instance Global Framework Agreements between global unions and transnational corporations. Fichter in this volume shows that, while they have a role to play, they cannot succeed in protecting labour rights in value chains unless the workers are empowered to make use of them and go beyond them. Otherwise they are, like fair trade,[6] a mere rubber stamp of good conscience for Western companies and consumers.

---

6. See the extensive 'Fair Trade, Employment and Poverty Reduction Research' conducted by SOAS, University of London, which is available at http://ftepr.org/about/.

Empowerment involves understanding complex phenomena so that struggles can be informed and, ultimately, successful. Strategic and independent analysis is what the GLC offers by drawing on critical and rigorous research on important phenomena. Such knowledge is key but must be leveraged in real struggles to change the world; otherwise it will have been in vain.

References

Bourdieu, P. (2000) 'Pour un savoir engagé', *Le Monde diplomatique*, February. English version available at: http://umintermediai501.blogspot.com/2008/09/for-engaged-knowledge-pour-un-savoir.html.

Hardt, M. and Negri, T. (2005) *Multitude: War and Democracy in the Age of Empire*, London: Penguin.

Piketty, T. (2014) *Capital in the Twenty-First Century*, Cambridge (Mass): Harvard University Press.

Shaxson, N. (2011) *Treasure Islands: Tax Havens and the Men who Stole the World*, London: Random House.

Stuckler, D. & S. Basu (2013) *The Body Economic: Why Austerity Kills*, New York: Basic Books.

Van der Walt, L. (2014) 'Politics at a Distance from the State: Speech to South African Movements', *Anarcho-Syndicalist Review* (ASR) 61, 21–3.

Understanding the Crisis

1

Planet Earth is Wage-led!

A Simultaneous Increase in the Profit Share by 1 Per Cent-point in the Major Developed and Developing Countries Leads to a 0.36 Per Cent Decline in Global GDP

Özlem Onaran

The dramatic decline in the share of wages in GDP in both the developed and developing world during the neoliberal era of the post-1980s has accompanied lower growth rates at the global level as well as in many countries. Mainstream economics continue to guide policy towards further wage moderation along with austerity as one of the major responses to the Great Recession. In our report for the International Labour Office (Onaran and Galanis, 2012), we show the vicious cycle generated by this race to the bottom. The main caveat of this wisdom is to treat wages as a cost item. However, wages have a dual role affecting not just costs but also demand. We work with a post-Keynesian/post-Kaleckian model, which allows this dual role.

A fall in the wage share has both negative and positive effects

We estimate the effect of a change in income distribution on aggregate demand (i.e. on consumption, investment, and net exports) in the G20 countries. Consumption is a function of wage and profit income, and is expected to decrease when the wage share decreases. Investment is estimated as a function of the profit share as well as demand, and a higher profitability is expected to stimulate investment for a given level of aggregate demand. Finally, exports and imports are estimated as functions of relative prices, which in turn are functions of nominal unit labour costs, closely related to the wage share. The total effect of the decrease in the wage share on aggregate demand depends on the relative size of the reactions of consumption, investment and net exports. If the total effect is negative, the demand regime is called wage-led; otherwise the regime is profit-led. Mainstream economic policy assumes that economies are always profit-led, whereas in the post-Keynesian models the relationship between the wage share and demand is an empirical matter, and depends on the structural characteristics of the economy.

Next, we develop a global model to calculate the effects of a simultaneous decline in wage share. We calculate the responses of each country to changes in domestic income distribution and to trade partners' wage share. The results are summarised in Table 1.1.

Three important findings emerge. First, domestic private demand (i.e. the sum of consumption and investment in Columns A and B in Table 1.1) is wage-led in all countries, because consumption is much more sensitive to an increase in the profit share than is investment. Second, foreign trade forms only a small part of aggregate demand in large countries, and therefore the positive effects of a decline in the wage share on net exports (Column C) do not suffice to offset the negative effects on domestic demand. Similarly, in the euro area as a whole, the private demand regime is wage-led. Finally, even if there are some countries, which are profit-led, the planet earth as a whole is wage-led. A simultaneous wage cut in a highly integrated global economy leaves most countries with only the negative domestic demand effects, and the global economy contracts. Furthermore some profit-led countries contract when they decrease their wage-share, if a similar strategy is implemented also by their trading partners. Beggar-thy-neighbour policies cancel out the competitiveness advantages in each country and are counter-productive. ILO (2012:60) in the *Global Wage Report 2012/13* writes 'the world economy as a whole is a closed economy. If competitive wage cuts or wage moderation policies are pursued simultaneously in a large number of countries, competitive gains will cancel out and the regressive effect of global wage cuts on consumption could lead to a worldwide depression of aggregate demand.'

At the national level, the US, Japan, the UK, the Euro area, Germany, France, Italy, Turkey and Korea are wage-led. Canada and Australia are the only developed countries that are profit-led; in these small open economies, distribution has a large effect on net exports (see Columns D and E). Argentina, Mexico, China, India, and South Africa are also profit-led.

Table 1 Summary of the effects of a 1%–point increase in the profit share (a decline in the wage share) at the national and global level

| | The effect of a 1%–point increase in the profit share in only one country on | | | | | The effect of a simultaneous 1%–point increase in the profit share on % change in aggregate demand |
	Consumption/ GDP *A*	Investment/ GDP *B*	Net exports/ GDP *C*	Initial change in private demand/GDP *D (A+B+C)*	% change in aggregate demand (D*multiplier) *E*	*F*
Euro area–12	-0.439	0.299	0.057	-0.084	-0.133	-0.245
Germany	-0.501	0.376	0.096	-0.029	-0.031	–
France	-0.305	0.088	0.198	-0.020	-0.027	–
Italy	-0.356	0.130	0.126	-0.100	-0.173	–
United Kingdom	-0.303	0.120	0.158	-0.025	-0.030	-0.214
United States	-0.426	0.000	0.037	-0.388	-0.808	-0.921
Japan	-0.353	0.284	0.055	-0.014	-0.034	-0.179
Canada	-0.326	0.182	0.266	0.122	0.148	-0.269
Australia	-0.256	0.174	0.272	0.190	0.268	0.172
Turkey	-0.491	0.000	0.283	-0.208	-0.459	-0.717
Mexico	-0.438	0.153	0.381	0.096	0.106	-0.111
Korea	-0.422	0.000	0.359	-0.063	-0.115	-0.864
Argentina	-0.153	0.015	0.192	0.054	0.075	-0.103
China	-0.412	0.000	1.986	1.574	1.932	1.115
India	-0.291	0.000	0.310	0.018	0.040	-0.027
South Africa	-0.145	0.129	0.506	0.490	0.729	0.390

Source: Onaran and Galanis, 2012.

Race to the bottom leads to lower global growth

At the global level, the race to the bottom in the wage share, i.e. simultaneous increase in the profit share by 1 per cent-point in the major developed and developing countries, leads to a 0.36 per cent decline in global GDP. The euro area, the UK, and Japan contract by 0.18–0.25 per cent and the US contracts by 0.92 per cent as a result of a simultaneous decline in the wage share (see Column F in Table 1.1). Some profit-led countries, specifically Canada, India, Argentina and Mexico, also contract as a result of this race to the bottom. The expansionary effects of a pro-capital redistribution of income in these countries are reversed when relative competitiveness effects are reduced as all countries implement a similar low wage competition strategy; this consequently leads to a fall in the GDP of the rest of the world. The wage-led economies contract more strongly in the case of a race to the bottom. Australia, South Africa and China are the only three countries that can continue to grow despite a simultaneous decline in the wage share.

The microeconomic rationale of pro-capital redistribution conflicts with the macroeconomic outcomes

First, at the national level in a wage-led economy, a higher profit share leads to lower demand and growth; thus even though a higher profit share at the firm level seems to be beneficial to individual capitalists, at the macroeconomic level a generalised fall in the wage share generates a problem of realisation of profits due to deficient demand. Second, even if increasing profit share seems to be promoting growth at the national level in the profit-led countries, at the global level a simultaneous fall in the wage share leads to global demand deficiency and lower growth.

Policy implications

At the national level, if a country is wage-led, pro-capital redistribution of income is detrimental to growth. There is room for policies to decrease income inequality without hurting the growth potential of the economies.

For the large wage-led economic areas with a high intra-regional trade and low extra-regional trade, like the euro area, macroeconomic and wage policy coordination can improve growth and employment. The wage moderation policy of the euro area is not conducive to growth.

Debt-led consumption, enabled by financial deregulation and housing bubbles seemed to offer a short-term solution to aggregate demand deficiency caused by falling wage share in countries like the US, UK, Spain or Ireland until the crisis. The current account deficits and debt in these countries were matched by an export-led model and current account surpluses of countries like Germany, or Japan, where exports had to compensate for the decline in domestic demand due to the fall in labour's share. However this model also proved to be unsustainable as it could only co-exist with imbalances in the other European countries – an issue, which is now in the epicentre of the euro crisis.

A global wage-led recovery as a way out of the global recession is economically feasible. Growth and an improvement in equality are consistent. This is true for wage-led and profit-led countries. We present a scenario, where all countries can grow along with an improvement in the wage share, and the global GDP would increase by 3.05 per cent (Onaran and Galanis, 2012).

The austerity policies with further detrimental effects on the wage shares since 2010 will only bring further stagnation. Growth in China and a few developing countries alone cannot be the locomotive of global growth.

A global wage-led recovery can also create space for domestic demand-led and egalitarian growth strategies rather than export orientation based on low wages in the developing countries. Second, even if some important developing countries are profit-led, like China and South Africa, south–south cooperation can create a large economic area, where destructive wage competition policies are avoided.

Rebalancing growth via increasing domestic demand in the major developing countries, in particular China would also be helpful in addressing global imbalances. However, this rebalancing can only take place in an international environment where the developed countries not only leave space for developmentalist policies, support technology transfer, but also create an expansionary global environment.

Given the profit-led structures in some developing countries, the solution requires a step forward by some large developed economies in terms of radically reversing the pro-capital distribution policies.

References

International Labour Organisation (2012) *Global Wage Report 2012/13*, International Labour Office. Available from www.ilo.org.
Onaran, Ö. and Galanis, G. (2012) 'Is aggregate demand wage-led or profit-led? National and global effects', Conditions of Work and Employment Series No. 40, International Labour Office. Available from www.ilo.org.

2

From Financial Crisis to Stagnation: The Destruction of Shared Prosperity and the Role of Economics

Thomas I. Palley

Marshall McLuhan, the famed philosopher of media, wrote: 'We shape our tools and they in turn shape us.' His insight also applies to the economy which is shaped significantly by economic policy derived from economic ideas. The critical role of economic policy and ideas is central to understanding the continuing global economic crisis which is the product of flawed policies derived from flawed ideas.

Competing perspectives on the crisis

Broadly speaking, there exists three different perspectives on the crisis. Perspective #1 is the hardcore neoliberal position, which can be labelled the '*government failure hypothesis*'. In the US it is identified with the Republican Party and the Chicago school of economics. Perspective #2 is the softcore neoliberal position, which can be labelled the '*market failure hypothesis*'. It is identified with the Obama administration, half of the Democratic Party, and the MIT economics departments. In Europe it is identified with Third Way politics. Perspective #3 is the progressive position which can be labelled the '*destruction of shared prosperity hypothesis*'. It is identified with the other half of the Democratic Party and the labour movement, but it has no standing within major economics departments owing to their suppression of alternatives to orthodox theory.

The government failure argument holds that the crisis is rooted in the US housing bubble and bust which was due to failure of monetary policy and government intervention in the housing market. With regard to monetary policy, the Federal Reserve pushed interest rates too low for too long in the prior recession. With regard to the housing market, government intervention drove up house prices by encouraging homeownership beyond peoples' means. The hardcore perspective therefore characterises the crisis as essentially a US phenomenon.

The softcore neoliberal market failure argument holds that the crisis is due to inadequate financial regulation. First, regulators allowed excessive risk-taking by banks. Second, regulators allowed perverse incentive pay structures within banks that encouraged management to engage in 'loan pushing' rather than 'good lending'. Third, regulators pushed both deregulation and self-regulation too far. Together, these failures contributed to financial misallocation, including misallocation of foreign saving provided through the trade deficit. The softcore perspective is therefore more global but it views the crisis as essentially a financial phenomenon.

The progressive 'destruction of shared prosperity' argument holds if the crisis is rooted in the neoliberal economic paradigm that has guided economic policy for the past 30 years. Although the US is the epicentre of the crisis, all countries are implicated as they all adopted the paradigm. That paradigm infected finance via inadequate regulation and via faulty incentive pay arrangements, but financial market regulatory failure was just one element.

The neoliberal economic paradigm was adopted in the late 1970s and early 1980s. For the period 1945–75 the US economy was characterised by a 'virtuous circle' Keynesian model built on full employment and wage growth tied to productivity growth. The model is illustrated in Figure 2.1. Productivity growth drove wage growth, which in turn fuelled demand growth and created full employment. That provided an incentive for investment, which drove further productivity growth and supported higher wages. This model held in the US and, subject to local modifications, it also held throughout the global economy – in Western Europe, Canada, Japan, Mexico, Brazil and Argentina.

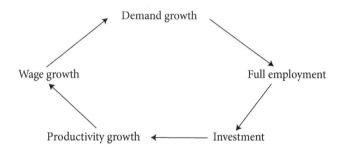

Figure 2.1   The 1945–75 virtuous circle Keynesian growth model

After 1980 the virtuous circle Keynesian model was replaced by a neoliberal growth model that severed the link between wages and productivity growth and created a new economic dynamic. Before 1980, wages were the engine of US demand growth. After 1980, debt and asset price inflation became the engine.

The new model is rooted in neoliberal economics and can be described as a neoliberal policy box that fences workers in and pressures them from all sides. It is illustrated in Figure 2.2. Corporate globalisation put workers in international competition via global production networks supported by free trade agreements and capital mobility. The 'small' government agenda attacked the legitimacy of government and pushed for deregulation regardless of dangers. The labour market flexibility agenda attacked unions and labour market supports such as the minimum wage, unemployment benefits, and employment protections. Finally, the abandonment of full employment created employment insecurity and weakened worker bargaining power.

This model was implemented on a global basis, in both North and South, which multiplied its impact. That explains the significance of the Washington Consensus which was enforced in Latin America, Africa, and former Communist countries by the International Monetary Fund and World Bank by making financial assistance conditional on adopting neoliberal policies.

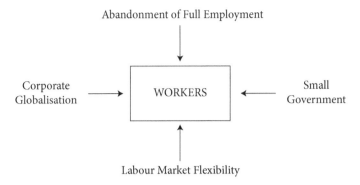

Figure 2.2 The neoliberal policy box

The new model created a growing 'demand gap' by gradually undermining the income and demand generation process. The role of finance was to fill that gap. Within the US, deregulation, financial innovation, and speculation enabled finance to fill the demand gap by lending to consumers and spurring asset price inflation. US consumers in turn filled the global demand gap.

Implications of different explanations

These three different perspectives make clear what is at stake as each recommends its own different policy response. For hardcore neoliberal government failure proponents the recommended policy response is to double-down on neoliberal policies by further deregulating financial and labour markets; deepening Central Bank independence and the commitment to low inflation; and further limiting government via fiscal austerity.

For softcore neoliberal market failure proponents the recommended policy response is to tighten financial regulation but continue with all other aspects of the existing neoliberal policy paradigm. That means continued support for corporate globalisation, so-called labour market flexibility, low inflation targeting, and fiscal austerity.

For proponents of the destruction of shared prosperity hypothesis the policy response is fundamentally different. The challenge is to overthrow the neoliberal paradigm and replace it with a 'structural Keynesian' paradigm that repacks the policy box and restores the link between wage and productivity growth. The structural Keynesian model is illustrated in

Figure 2.3. The goal is to take workers out of the box and put corporations and financial markets in so that they are made to serve the broader public interest. That requires replacing corporate globalisation with managed globalisation; restoring commitment to full employment; replacing the neoliberal anti-government agenda with a social democratic government agenda; replacing the neoliberal labour market flexibility with a solidarity-based labour market agenda.

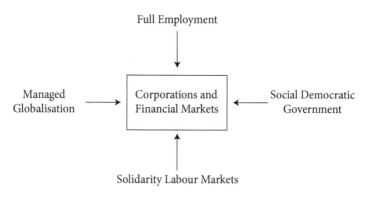

Figure 2.3   The structural Keynesian box

Managed globalisation means a world with labour standards, coordinated exchange rates, and managed capital flows. A social democratic agenda means government ensuring adequate provision of social safety nets, fundamental needs such as healthcare and education, and secure retirement incomes. A solidarity-based labour market means balanced bargaining power between workers and corporations which involves union representation, adequate minimum wages and unemployment insurance, and appropriate employee rights and protections. Lastly, since the neoliberal model was adopted globally, there is a need to recalibrate the global economy. This is where the issue of 'global rebalancing' enters and emerging market economies need to shift away from export-led growth strategies to domestic demand-led strategies.

According to the destruction of share prosperity hypothesis, failure to repack the policy box and recalibrate the global economy means the global economy will remain beset by income inequality, demand shortage and race-to-the bottom pressures. That toxic combination inevitably generates stagnation.

Conclusion: ideas matter

The essential insight from the above discussion is that each perspective carries its own policy prescriptions. Consequently, the explanation which prevails will strongly impact the course of economic policy. That places economics at the centre of the political struggle as it influences which explanation prevails.

More than seven years after the financial crisis of 2008, the economics profession still remains split between the hardcore and softcore neoliberal positions. However, even if the profession's fundamental thinking remains little changed, the unpleasant reality of economic conditions has enabled the arguments of the shared prosperity hypothesis to gain greater prominence. This is evident in growing mainstream chatter about the possibility of stagnation and the potential importance of income distribution for full employment and growth.

So far that chatter is skin deep and has not impacted economic policy or teaching, but that too can change under the pressure of an ugly reality that produces mass political demand for real change. The Great Depression of the 1930s forced economics to change and provided an opening for Keynesian economics. The Great Recession and the current stagnation may eventually force contemporary mainstream economics to change.

The one certainty is that change will be politically contested as powerful elites and orthodox economists have an interest in preserving the dominance of the existing paradigm by ensuring their explanation of the Great Recession prevails. That makes it essential that unions engage the theoretical debate regarding the causes of the crisis and how economies work. Their political muscle is needed and the outcome of that debate is critical to their own existence and success.

References

Palley, T. (2012) *From Financial Crisis to Stagnation: The Destruction of Shared Prosperity and the Role of Economics* (Cambridge: Cambridge University Press).

3

State Funding of Research and the Narrowing of Economics in the United Kingdom

Frederic Sterling Lee

In 1986, the United Kingdom instituted an exercise through which the allocation of state research funds to universities and their departments was based on the quality of the research they produced. While the official justification for the exercise was the need to be selective in the allocation of limited research funds, the non-talked about agenda behind the exercise was to reduce the number of research universities to a manageable number and to ensure that these elite universities conducted research and carried out teaching that was consistent with the interests of the economic and political elite which control the state. Consequently the ensuing research selectivity exercise, known as the Research Assessment Exercise (RAE) was and is popular with the Tories, New Labour, and anybody else who believes that the State should have quasi-direct and complete control over the thinking and research activities of its citizens.

Most academics initially thought the exercise would be a fair way of allocating state research funding when the state decided to reduce its commitment to higher education. However, in some disciplines, such as economics, it became evident by the mid-1990s that the exercise was also being used to cleanse economic departments of heterodox economic ideas that did not conform to mainstream (neoclassical) economic theory and with the neoliberal, pro-market policies based on the theory and which the state approved of. But the precise manner through which the cleansing process operated was not clearly understood. The rest of the chapter deals with the cleansing process, its consequences for UK economics, and what can be done about it.

Cleansing of UK economics

It is now possible to see how the process worked. In a somewhat synchronised manner, the Royal Economics Society under the direction of the state-organised RAE recommended mainstream economists for the economics panel; these economists in turn made decisions about the quality of the research output submitted by the economics departments; these decisions in turn determined the research funding allocated to the departments; and upon discovering the apparent basis of what is considered quality research – that is publications in a specific group of mainstream journals called the Diamond List journals – UK economics departments then directed if not harassed their staff to publish in them (and if not got them transferred to other departments or made their working conditions so bad that they left the university) and only hired mainstream economists who could publish in them. The outcome of these mutually reinforcing relationships is that, over time, heterodox economics is mostly eliminated from UK economics, economics departments became increasingly homogeneous both internally and with respect to other departments, mainstream economics research gets concentrated in fewer but quite acceptable areas that are compatible with the economic and political interests of the state (as noted above), and a few mainstream economics departments dominate UK economics.

Outcomes

What is the concrete meaning of these outcomes? First of all, over 75 per cent of all research funding goes to just 13 universities; and these same universities teach only mainstream economics to their students and only hire mainstream economists. However, these latter outcomes are not just specific to them. Because all economics departments (whether engaged in research or not) feel the pressure to be mainstream, heterodox economists are not hired, resulting in a majority of UK economics departments having no heterodox economists on staff, and not teaching any alternative economics to their students. This means that most UK students who take economics as their first degree are not introduced to any alternative economic theories or policies; an outcome that is reinforced by the state's decree through its benchmark statement for economics which says that only mainstream economics should be taught to students.

The result of this cleansing of UK economics of heterodox economists and their ideas is to create a single national view of what constitutes both economics and appropriate economic policies, such as cuts to government spending so as to deliberately create unemployment, eliminating help for the poor because they brought their poverty upon themselves and the unemployed because they brought it upon themselves by being inefficient workers, privatising health care, and attacking trade unions and all other forms of support for living wages and safe working conditions. These policies emanate directly from the mainstream economic theory taught to students as a faith-based truth. So it seems that the state, through the RAE, has bought the economics and economic policies that it desired. But there is more, in that students and the UK population at large are deliberately prevented from developing critical thinking so that they can, on their own, evaluate different economic theories and their associated economic policies and determine which one they think is best. In short, the state through the RAE has made mainstream economists the direct enforcers of national thought control in economics.

What is to be done?

So what is the way forward? The first is, do not trust economists and their economic policies; second, do not think that academic economists give unbiased advice; and lastly, do not give economists associated with elite universities, such as the London School of Economics, University College London, the University of Oxford and the University of Cambridge, any respect as their economics is designed to support the 1 per cent and at the same time make the lives of at least the lower 90 per cent worse off. There are, moreover, more positive steps that must be taken at the same time. The first is engaging in political action directed at the state-sponsored RAE to shut it down; and at the same time put pressure on the state to eliminate subject benchmarking which prescribes what is the acceptable subject matter for an academic discipline – much like telling people what religious views they must believe and how to carry out their religious activities. For example, subject benchmarking in economics defines economics as only mainstream economics; consequently Marxian economics and any other kind of heterodox economics is not economics and cannot be included in the study of economics. In addition, departments that promote pluralism in the teaching of economics and heterodox economists need financial support to stay viable and carry out research that supports the other 90 per cent.

It is obvious that the business community bought their way into universities by providing funds to build business schools and establishing professorial chairs in business; and the same has been done in other areas such as the pharmaceutical and biological sciences. Moreover, there are even specific instances, in the United States for example, where conservative neoliberal foundations and business people have attempted to redirect the teaching of economics in economics departments to support their free-market ideology (for example Florida State University). So, in light of this 'acceptable' activity to push economics in a particular direction, similar efforts need to be made. For example, find economics departments that provide their students with a pluralist understanding of economics and support them through providing student scholarships or even just by encouraging students to do their economics degree in the department. In addition, all heterodox economists need financial support to carry out their research. Since the state and reputable foundations will not generally support heterodox economists and their research, such support has to come from individuals and from trade unions and progressive charitable organisations – hence pressure needs to be put on them to provide such support. Moreover, alternative, non-state based 'schools' providing a pluralist approach to economics need to be established and promoted, such as something like an independent working-class education movement devoted specifically to economics.

Finally, to force the spectre of heterodox economics to be acknowledged by mainstream economists, it is necessary for heterodox economists to take a more active, confrontational route, such as disrupting the Royal Economics Society annual conference. Each of the positive suggestions takes time, unpaid effort and money, but given the current dominance of the state and mainstream economics, there is no other course of action.

References

Lee, F. S., Pham, X. and Gu, G. (2013) 'The UK Research Assessment Exercise and the Narrowing of UK Economics', *Cambridge Journal of Economics*, Vol. 37, No. 4.

4

Globalisation and Taxation: Trends and Consequences

Ilan Strauss

Taxes allow government to sustain a healthy economy

To misuse Marx's often quoted phrase: governments are in love with tax revenue but 'the course of true love never did run smooth'. Having a healthy tax collection is just one of the vital links in the post-Second World War 'economic consensus' which has been undermined by growing global integration and technological change, and an institutional and legal set-up which has failed to keep pace with these developments. These pressures have led the OECD to begin work on reforming the global tax system in an effort to tackle base erosion and profit shifting (BEPS). Below we explore why BEPS is happening, its consequences, and possible remedies.[1]

Tax revenue is important for several reasons: it allows governments to implement fiscal policy and achieve important societal goals, such as reducing poverty and inequality. This occurs through expanding education and other essential services as well as through transfers. After the benefits of tax and welfare are taken into consideration, 'market poverty' in Northern European OECD economies declines by around three quarters, whereas in

---

1. Tax comparisons are sensitive to what statistic is being used (statutory, effective, or marginal tax rates) and if it is weighted or unweighted (for indexes). All data here comes from OECD Stat, unless stated otherwise.

the US poverty declines by only one-quarter. Historically, Thomas Piketty and his colleagues detail how the extension of progressive income taxation and taxation of inheritances made it more difficult for the rich to maintain their wealth. This is important given recent evidence by the IMF and the World Bank that high levels of inequality are harmful for growth.

Globalisation has had several notable impacts on tax rates and tax collection

Firstly, average OECD income tax rates have fallen for corporations and individuals, as detailed in *Trends in Top Incomes and their Taxation in OECD Countries* (Förster et al., 2014). The average OECD statutory top personal income tax rate declined from 66 per cent in 1981 to 42 per cent in 2010; average statutory OECD corporate income tax rates declined from 47 per cent in 1981 to 25.5 per cent in 2012; OECD top marginal tax rates on dividends fell from 75 per cent in 1981 to 42.5 per cent in 2011; while taxes on wealth and inheritance have been reduced or abolished in many OECD countries. Declining tax progressivity has been accompanied by rising inequality: the same study finds a strong negative correlation between top marginal tax rates and the pre-tax shares of top incomes across OECD countries.

Declining tax rates reflects growing global tax competition. Global economic integration has made the tax rate an 'externality': When firms relocate among jurisdictions (or countries) in response to differences in the after-tax profit rate, the level of employment in one jurisdiction is determined not only by its own tax rate but by the tax rates of other jurisdictions.

Secondly, globalisation has ushered in a destructive incentives competition to attract and retain capital. The mobility of capital has given it leverage over immobile governments desperate to expand employment and output. This has led to an explosion of (often unnecessary and harmful) incentives offered by governments to businesses in an effort to woo them to their jurisdiction. After accounting for the vast array of tax benefits which businesses receive, the effective tax rate paid by corporations is usually substantially below the statutory rates. This can be a form of 'harmful tax practice', argues the OECD. The EU regulates the use of such incentives under

State Aid laws to ensure that incentives are offered only when necessary and in proportion to the developmental needs of the region or sector.

Thirdly, tax revenue has grown in importance for most OECD countries, partly due to higher levels of unemployment and a greater portion of pensioners requiring support. Even with the rise of free-market economics, state expenditure as a percentage of GDP has trended upwards in the US and the euro area, peaking in 2009 at 43 per cent and 50 per cent respectively.[2] In order to try and keep up, tax revenue to GDP has on average increased continuously in OECD countries – but only until 2000, after which it stagnates returning to the previous peak of 34 per cent only in 2013.

Fourthly, the tax burden on wages (as opposed to capital income) is rising in OECD countries. This is despite the profit share increasing in most economies. Income tax has always been the mainstay of tax revenue, which falls disproportionately on salary and wage earners. Even countries with relatively larger welfare states tax consumption and labour incomes more heavily to raise the extra funds. In the past this wage bias in taxation has been due to not wanting to 'kill the goose which lays the golden egg', i.e. to reduce investment by eating into corporate profits. More recently, the mobility of capital is exerting an influence on the composition of tax revenues.

Working around the tax system

The challenges facing today's tax system are driven by the mobility of capital and wealth, the growing international division of labour, and how firms in the digital economy make profits and add 'value'.

Historically, as states began to inconsistently tax individuals and companies according to their residence as well as according to where the source of their income arose, tax treaties were created to ensure that double taxation and double non-taxation did not occur. Today legal tax planning leverages double taxation rules to facilitate double non-taxation of corporate profits; while tax havens are used to house profits and reduce tax bills. The digital economy further complicates matters as large portions of corporate profits now rest in intangible assets, which inherited tax law does not deal with adequately.

---

2. However, there was substantial variability between countries and volatility. Between 1995 and 2013 G7 countries' average expenditure to GDP was roughly unchanged (equal weighting given to each country), but during this period the trend fell and rose by more than 15 per cent.

Three common methods are used to reduce a company's tax bill: (1) special purpose entities (SPEs); (2) 'hybrids'; and (3) abusive transfer pricing. We discuss each briefly.

SPEs are entities with no or few employees and are used as vehicles for holding activities or group financing. Foreign direct investments may be channelled through tax havens such as Luxembourg using them. Hybrid mismatch arrangements aim to have the same money or transaction treated differently by different countries. A common feature of such arrangements is dual tax residence of a company. The most 'successful' hybrids achieve double non-taxation.

Transfer pricing is the setting of a price for goods and services sold between related entities within an enterprise; for example, one subsidiary of Amazon paying another for use of the brand. The cost of such a transaction should mirror the one that Amazon would charge an unrelated entity (the 'arm's length' price), but in practise this is difficult to define. Abusive transfer pricing is used to shift costs, and in turn profits, to jurisdictions that minimises the tax bill. Around 60 per cent of world trade takes place within multinational enterprises making the use of abusive transfer pricing commonplace and particularly destructive.

Tax abuses using these tools and various loopholes are common: Amazon generated online sales of more than £3.3 billion in Britain in 2011 but paid no corporate tax on any of the profits from that income. Google reduced its effective overseas corporate tax rate to just 2.4 per cent by 2010. The impact of such practises on developing economies is particularly pernicious since a larger portion of their capital stock is foreign owned and they have a narrower tax base.

Note that such practises, and in particular abusive transfer pricing, cannot be captured by the majority of capital flight statistics that look, in part, for differences in the trade receipts used by exporting and importing partner countries. Under abusive transfer pricing the trade receipts will be the same at both ends, just uniformly too high or too low.

The way forward

Coordination between states is central to reducing aggressive tax planning and tax competition.

The OECD has begun a series of important reforms focused around a 15-point action plan. It includes measures to: deal adequately with the digital economy, neutralise the effects of hybrids, prevent the abuse of tax treaties through 'treaties shopping', strengthen controlled foreign companies (CFC) rules, limit base erosion via interest deductions and other financial payments, develop a multilateral instrument to amend bilateral tax treaties, and reduce harmful transfer pricing by ensuring (among other things) that companies report on a country-by-country basis certain key information. Underlying such actions is a push for far greater information sharing and transparency to facilitate the free exchange of financial information. These measures are already impacting the global tax system positively, but remain reliant on the voluntary cooperation of governments.

An additional suggestion is to develop a *unitary taxation system* to remove the incentives facing TNCs to shift their tax burden to more favourable tax regimes (Picciotto, 2007). This would mean that instead of related companies being treated and taxed as separate entities, they would be taxed as a single unit on their consolidated accounts. The total income and profits of a company would be calculated based on their combined global operations, with the tax revenue from this being apportioned to countries on the basis of an agreed upon formulae. Corporate taxation between states in the US is currently done on a unitary basis.

Lastly, Thomas Piketty has put a global wealth tax on the agenda. While noted as being unrealistic, mechanisms to establish a globally agreed and enforced wealth tax could be one of the most useful avenues for dealing in the future with some of the flaws in the current tax system and concurrently reducing inequality. At present net wealth is taxed in only a few OECD countries (France, Norway, the Netherlands, Spain and Switzerland), and only on particular assets over a certain amount.

References

Förster, M., Llena-Nozal, A., and Nafilyan, V. (2014) *Trends in Top Incomes and their Taxation in OECD Countries*, OECD Social, Employment and Migration Working Papers, No. 159. Available from www.oecd.org.

Love, P. (2012) 'How to Pay Less Tax', *OECD Insights*. Available from www.oecd.org.

Love, P. (2013) 'BEPS: Why You're Taxed More than a Multinational', *OECD Insights*. Available from www.oecd.org.

OECD (2013) *Action Plan on Base Erosion and Profit Shifting*. Available from www.oecd.org.

Picciotto, S. (2007) 'The International Crisis of Income Taxation: Combating Tax Havens, Capital Flight and Corruption', Presentation to Critical Legal Conference (Kent, UK), February.

Saint Amans, P. (2014) 'Combating BEPS and Making Sure we have Fair Tax Systems: An OECD/G20 Venture', *OECD Insights*. Available from www.oecd. org.

5

T-shirt Economics: Labour in the Imperialist World Economy

Tony Norfield

Everybody knows that workers in developed capitalist countries are paid more than those in poorer countries. However, the divergence in average wages can nevertheless be surprising: not just 20 per cent or 50 per cent, but more like a factor of 2, 5, 10 or 20 between the richer countries and the poorer countries (see Norfield, 2012 and 2014). Mainstream economic theory explains this – and justifies it – by arguing that workers in richer countries are more productive than in poorer ones, because the former are more educated and skilled, working with higher levels of technology. Yet this explanation does not sit well with the reality that many manufacturing employees in poor countries are employed, directly or indirectly, by major corporations, and working with technology that is often comparable to that in the richer countries.

An American manufacturing worker on some $36 per hour, including welfare and other benefits, may not feel rich, and is certainly earning a tiny proportion of the salary of the managers and the CEO. Nevertheless, this is more than three times what a Brazilian manufacturing worker earns, more than five times the wages and benefits of a Mexican worker, more than 10 times for a worker in China, 17 times for a worker in the Philippines, and an even bigger multiple of what is called labour 'compensation' for workers in India and Bangladesh.[3]

The difference in wages has little to do with different national living costs. Even if it did, this would not be relevant for the argument that wage differences are based on productivity. The World Bank and others calculate 'purchasing power parity' values for GDP to indicate that a lower wage than in the US, for example $5, may be able to buy the equivalent of $10 or $15 of goods purchased by workers in the US. However, this does little to explain the huge gap in earnings. Neither do productivity differences look like a good explanation. The technology used in poor countries to assemble computers, make clothing and perform other manufacturing operations is not a screwdriver or a pair of scissors, with the work done in a shed that has no electricity supply. Companies such as Foxconn have vast production complexes, one employing some 400,000 workers in 15 factories in China.[4]

This kind of operation is more typical of today's international supply chains for major corporations than one where poor countries use backward technology and have far lower productivity. Economic data for a poor country may suggest very low productivity, but this will reflect the economy as a whole, often including a mass of small-scale farming and subsistence activities. It will not be true for the sectors in which imperialist firms have invested or to which they have supply links, and on which they depend for their cheap goods.

It is widely known that US corporate giant Apple depends on low-wage suppliers in Asia. In the case of the iPhone 4, total supplies per unit, including flash memory and processing chips, are reported to have cost around $188, while labour assembly costs in China (at the infamous Foxconn factory) were less than $7 per unit (See Barboza 2010 and Chamberlain, 2011). Yet the iPhone was retailing in the US at $600. Is it really the case that the remaining $400 or so is 'value added' by Apple? Or might it have more

---

3. Wage compensation data in 2013 are taken from Conference Board 2014. Note that the US compensation level is taken as the base line, but a number of countries in North-western Europe, and also Australia, had compensation levels above those in the US.

4. Chinese wage levels have risen sharply in recent years, prompting Foxconn, etc., to greatly expand the use of robotics. Chinese manufacturing wages and benefits have increased compared to those in the US, due to labour shortages, but remain at around 10 per cent of the US rate.

to do with Apple using its market power in buying and selling, as well as Foxconn's ultra-exploitation of its workers?

Unravelling exploitation

An investigative article in *Die Zeit* detailed the story for another, far less glamorous product: a T-shirt made in Bangladesh (Uchatius, 2010). The T-shirt story is typical for the goods imported into rich countries that are produced by workers in poor countries. It is also a telling example, because here there can be no obscuring of the key relationships by appealing to the superior techniques, productivity, design or specialist skills of the rich countries when explaining why so little of the final selling price of the T-shirt accrues to the manufacturer in the poor country. It is an example, in other words, of how rich countries *appropriate* value created in poor countries, even though mainstream economics would argue that the price received by the different agents of production reflects the value of what they are selling (Smith, 2010).[5]

In 2010, Swedish retailer Hennes & Mauritz (H&M) sold the T-shirt in Germany at €4.95. This is how the selling price was broken down in the stages from the cotton raw material to the shirt ending up in a bag at the shop sales desk (Uchatius, 2010):

- €0.40: cost of 400g of cotton raw material bought from the US by the factory in Bangladesh;
- €1.35: the price H&M paid per T-shirt to the Bangladeshi company;
- €1.41: after adding 6 cents per shirt for shipping costs to Hamburg in Germany;
- €3.40: after adding roughly €2 for transport in Germany, shop rent, sales force, marketing and administration in Germany;
- €4.16: after adding some other items plus around 60 cents net profit for H&M;
- €4.95: after adding 19 per cent VAT, paid to the German state.

---

5. John Smith explains the important question of value appropriated versus value created in his analysis of the global division of labour. He also makes a point, not dealt with here, that there is a division of labour in the world economy between highly competitive producers on low margins based in the 'South' and a more monopolistic market dominated by producers in the 'North', with competition limited by patents and other barriers.

The €4.95 for the T-shirt and the 60 cents profit per shirt are, of course, multiplied by the many millions: this is a mass-market business. The Bangladeshi factory makes 125,000 shirts per day, of which half are sold to H&M, the rest to other Western retailers. One worker at the factory, even after a 17 per cent pay rise, earned just €1.36 *per day*, based on a 10–12 hour day. The machine they work with produces a target of 250 T-shirts per hour.

Not enough information was given in *Die Zeit*'s article to work out the labour cost per T-shirt, including the other workers involved, but it is very much less than the 95 cents margin that the factory receives from H&M after the cost of the cotton (i.e. €1.35 minus €0.40). The 95 cents cover labour costs, power, the materials needed other than cotton, depreciation of machinery and other items, plus a margin for the local manufacturer's profit. Using one study on labour costs in Bangladesh's textile industry, official government data on wage and productivity trends in the cotton textile sector, plus exchange rate changes, leads to an estimate for the direct labour cost of a T-shirt produced in Bangladesh (in 2010) was around 2–3 cents, probably lower (Zohir cited in Absar, 2001).[6] Working instead from assumptions about the number of workers per machine, the daily wage paid and the daily output, an estimate for the direct labour cost would be lower still, at less than one cent. In any case, H&M's 60 cent profit margin was a huge multiple of what was paid to the workers in Bangladesh making the T-shirts! These calculations are far from exact, but they would have to be dramatically too low to make any appreciable difference to this extraordinary rate of exploitation.

Who gains from sweated labour?

Since 2010, there has been little sign that things have improved. This was exemplified by the April 2013 Rana Plaza disaster in the Dhaka area of

6. S.C. Zohir (cited in Absar 2001) estimates that the unit labour cost in 1994 of a 'shirt' in Bangladesh was 11 cents (in US currency). If the labour cost of a (full) shirt was 11 cents, presumably a T-shirt would cost less. I assume (a high) 8 cents for a T-shirt. I took exchange rates for the US dollar, euro and Bangladeshi taka from central bank sources. Data for cotton worker wages and productivity since 1994, including my own estimates, were from the Bangladesh Bureau of Statistics, 2010, Tables 5.05 and 10.18. The second labour cost calculation is based on assuming three workers per machine earning a total of €4.50 per day. If they produce 250 T-shirts per hour over ten hours, then that is 2,500 shirts per day, with an average direct labour cost of 0.18 cents per shirt. Other assumptions are possible, but all plausible ones lead to very low numbers.

Bangladesh, when a commercial building containing clothing factories collapsed and more than 1,100 workers lost their lives, with another 2,500 injured. The embarrassment to local capitalists and to their customers, the corporations of rich countries, helped secure a large wage increase for the workers, but the extra daily wage would not have paid for the morning cup of coffee that many people in richer countries buy from Starbucks. For some, especially the lower-paid women workers and the unskilled, their total daily wage would not even have afforded that 'luxury'.

Another striking feature of the T-shirt data is how such a large portion of the revenue from the shop's selling price goes to the state in taxes and to a wide range of workers, executives, landlords and businesses in Germany and, by implication, elsewhere. The cheap T-shirts and a wide range of other imported goods, produced by super-exploited workers in poor countries, are both affordable for consumers and an important source of income for the state. Their low wages are one reason why the richer countries can have lots of shop assistants, delivery drivers, managers and administrators, accountants, advertising executives, a wide range of welfare payments and much else besides. The wage rates in Bangladesh are particularly low, but even the multiples of these seen elsewhere point to the same conclusion: oppression of workers in the poorer countries gives direct economic benefits to the mass of people in the richer countries.

References

Absar, S.S. (2001) 'Problems Surrounding Wages: The Ready-Made Garments Sector in Bangladesh', *Labour and Management in Development*, Vol. 2, No. 7, Australian National University.

Bangladesh Bureau of Statistics (2010) *Statistical Yearbook of Bangladesh 2010*. Available from www.bbs.gov.bd/.

Barboza, D. (2010) 'Supply Chain for iPhone Highlights Costs in China', *New York Times*, 6 July. Available from www.nytimes.com.

Chamberlain, G. (2011) 'Apple Factories Accused of Exploiting Chinese Workers', 30 April. Available from www.theguardian.com.

Conference Board (2014) *International Comparisons of Hourly Compensation Costs in Manufacturing, 2013*, December.

Norfield, T. (2012) 'Stubborn Facts'. Available from http://economicsofimperialism.blogspot.co.uk.

Norfield, T. (2014) 'How Much Do Santa's Helpers Get Paid'. Available from http://economicsofimperialism.blogspot.co.uk.

Smith, J. (2010) *Imperialism & the Globalisation of Production*, PhD thesis. Available from www.mediafire.com/?5r339mnn4zmubq7.

Uchatius, W. (2010) 'Das Welthemd' ('The World Shirt'), *Die Zeit*, 17 December. Available from www.zeit.de.

Europe in Turmoil

6

Greece in the Deadlock of the Troika's Austerity Trap

Giorgos Argitis

In 2010 Greece was incapable of raising funds from the private bond markets to meet its financial commitments linked to its accumulated public debt. Greece's insolvency increased the possibility of sovereign default and the country sought and obtained financial assistance from the so-called 'Troika' – that is the International Monetary Fund, the European Central Bank and the European Commission. Section 2 argues that the failure of Greece's first and second adjustment programmes were caused by the adverse effects of misguided austerity programmes on the economy, given Greece's euro-area membership and its productive and institutional structures. Section 3 outlines an alternative policy for Greece to exit the crisis. Section 4 concludes.

The strategy of 'the Creditors': austerity and labour market flexibility

The arrival of 'the Creditors' in Greece in 2010 triggered an immediate switch to extreme austerity policies. The primary objectives of the first and second Memorandums of Economic and Financial Policies (May 2010 and March 2012 respectively) were to place Greece's public debt on a viable and sustainable path, to restore market confidence and access to the private credit markets and to create the foundations for sound medium-term growth. This economic policy was formulated according to three pillars: The first targeted the drastic reduction of the fiscal deficit that was equal to 14.5 per cent of GDP during the period 2010–14. To achieve this target, Greece had to take revenue and expenditure measures that amounted to 16 per cent of GDP. The extension of the adjustment period up to 2016 requires further measures that amount to 4 per cent of GDP. The first bailout programme focused on a considerable reduction of government expenditure, especially of pensions and public sector wages, together with an increase in tax rates and the privatisation of state enterprises.

The second pillar consisted of structural reforms that targeted domestic devaluation, which is considered vital to boost competitiveness, exports and economic growth. The second bailout programme contained specific structural reforms that were meant to free up Greece's 'rigid labour market' and reduce the minimum wage by more than 20 per cent. The third pillar aimed to preserve financial stability. Greek banks were seen as vulnerable to the downturn and to an adverse feedback loop from the sovereign crisis. The second adjustment programme also included €50 billion that would be available for the recapitalisation of Greek banks after the 2012 'haircut' of the sovereign debt. It is crucial to note that since 2008 the Greek banks have received a total amount of about €100 billion for their recapitalisation out of today's Greece's €320 billion public debt.

The implementation of the extreme austerity policies of the Troika's two Memoranda has had catastrophic consequences in an economy with structural productive deficits; in Greece, economic activity and employment are indeed heavily reliant on the growth of domestic demand (ILO, 2014). Today the size of the Greek economy is about *25 per cent below its 2008 level*. One in four jobs that existed before the crisis has been lost. The unemployment rate is close to 27 per cent, while it was 7.2 per cent at the end of 2008. More than 70 per cent of the unemployed have been without a job for more than one year, and almost half for more than two years. Of particular concern in this respect is youth unemployment, which stood at 56.7 per cent in the first quarter of 2014, and ranks as the highest in the EU. Note that youth unemployment was 21.3 per cent in 2008. Economic austerity has caused detrimental social effects. The number of emigrants has increased by 30 per cent between 2010 and 2012, while the at-risk-of-poverty rate has increased from slightly over 20 per cent in 2009 to almost 36 per cent in 2012.

The cherry on the cake is that the debt structure of the Greek public sector did not become sustainable after the 'haircut' in March 2012. Note that in 2010 the restructuring of Greece's unmanageable public debt was totally ruled out by the creditors in order to minimise the contagion risk in the eurozone. At the end of 2011, Troika realised that the first bailout failed to help Greece to place the government debt-to-GDP ratio on a sustainable path and to restore the country's solvency (see Argitis and Nikolaidi, 2014). In the beginning of 2012 Troika decided on a very ambiguous trimming of Greece's public debt that caused damaging effects on the stability of the Greek banking sector and the viability of the Greek public pension funds. As long as the Greek debt is considered to be unsustainable, liquidity and solvency problems arise, rapidly multiply, and spread to the entire economy, which continues to evolve through a 'debt-deflation' process.

An alternative strategy for Greece: employment and sound industrial relations

The macro, labour and social statistics of Greece are alarming. The current fiscal, financial and economic crisis necessitates a fundamental review of the prevailing Troika's neoliberal economic policy model. Overcoming recession, stagnation and unemployment is the most urgent task. To generate a strong recovery, we first need to stop the policies of fiscal austerity and of internal devaluation. Greece needs an alternative strategy that will promote a new, sustainable growth model that focuses on job creation. The essential pillars of a sustainable employment and growth strategy must be the following (Argitis, 2012):

- It is fundamental to revise the government's debt commitments according to the principle 'viable primary surplus – viable public debt' in order to restore Greece's solvency and credibility. It is important to create positive expectations that the Greek economy can generate primary surpluses that can fulfil its annual interest obligations. It is therefore crucial first to determine an economically and socially affordable primary surplus. The sustainability of primary surpluses depends heavily on economic growth and social stability. Any attempt to create primary surplus in a stagnant and depressed economy through economic austerity is bound to fail, with detrimental economic and social effects, without resolving the problems of solvency and credibility. As a result, a restructuring of the country's public debt should incorporate different interventions such as a 'haircut' of its nominal stock of debt, a close to zero interest rate and a considerable extension of the period in which Greece will have to meet its interest and principal payment agreements.

- Economic policy should stimulate domestic demand. Growth must be heavily rooted in employment and acknowledge the vital role of workers' rights and prosperity in the development process. Sustainable growth and a high level of employment create the best basis for reducing debt levels and budgeting sustainably. In doing this, a crucial step is the re-institutionalisation of sound industrial relations that, in the forms of collective bargaining, higher minimum wage and lower atypical employment, can advance and sustain domestic demand. Furthermore, a long-term investment plan is critical to improving productivity and competiveness. New European investment funds are vital to support sustainable growth in Greece.

- We must recognise that the private sector, even when not dragged down by austerity and liquidity shortages, cannot be expected to bring unemployment back to acceptable levels on its own. We need to think about new institutions and policies that match the scale of the current crisis and target directly the unemployment problem. Such a policy could be the institutionalisation of Hyman Minsky's 'Employer of Last Resort' programme (see Durand and Lang in this volume). Direct employment creation is a preferable macro-social policy response to the Troika's blind faith in the hypothetical employment effect of labour market flexibility and the gradual abolition of the minimum wage. This policy response can be promptly promoted in the form of 'Employment Guarantee Programmes' (EGP) aiming at channelling resources to targeted groups, such as youths and women, as well as to particular regions creating jobs in care and child development activities, environmental restoration and fire protection and social and healthcare services, which offer higher economic multipliers than traditional infrastructure public jobs (see Antonopoulos et al., 2014). The EGP could be financed by curtailing tax evasion and drawing on the primary surplus.

- Apart from institutional changes with immediate expansionary results, Greece also needs a new growth model. A long-term growth policy must strive for reforms to foster the transition to a new, export-oriented economy with higher structural competitiveness. Its success will hinge on changing the productive structure and re-allocating resources towards modern sectors such as green energy and organic agriculture, as well as to traditional, but competitive, industries such as the food industry. The most important developmental change for Greece is to change the dominant culture of entrepreneurship, which is geared towards taking advantage of redistributive mechanisms, such as tax evasion, social security contributions evasion, black labour and unpaid work, high mark-ups and price speculation financing conspicuous consumption. Instead, entrepreneurs ought to pursue profits from investing in R&D, expanding production, and market shares, and developing export-oriented activities targeting higher scales of capital accumulation.

Conclusion

Greece has fallen into an austerity-default trap that moves from a decline in domestic demand due to fiscal and income austerity to falling tax revenues, which undermine the country's ability to pay back its debt, increasing fears of government default. Deviations from the fiscal and growth targets elicit new rounds of Troika pressures for further austerity that undermine democracy. The austerity-default trap creates a vicious and self-defeating cycle that increases government's credit risk. This generates liquidity and solvency problems that hamper growth and employment possibilities. Greece needs a new policy strategy to promote employment and sound industrial relations in order to create viable growth conditions for restoring its sovereign solvency. This will require a break from Troika-imposed neoliberalism.

References

Antonopoulos, R., Adam, S., Kijong, K., Masterson, T. and Papadimitriou, D. (2014) 'Responding to the Unemployment Challenge: A Job Guarantee Proposal for Greece', Research Project Report, The Levy Economics Institute of Bard College and the Observatory of Economic and Social Developments, Labour Institute, Greek General Confederation of Labour, Annandale-on-Hudson, June.

Argitis, G. (2012) *Default and Economic Crisis. Failure and Collapse of the Greek Model of Capitalism* (in Greek) (Athens: Alexandria).

Argitis, G. and Nikolaidi, M. (2014) 'The financial fragility and the crisis of the Greek government sector: A Minskian analysis', *International Review of Applied Economics*, Vol. 28, No. 3.

International Labour Organisation (ILO) (2014) *Productive Jobs for Greece.* (Geneva: ILO).

7

The ECB's Misleading Understanding of the Euro Crisis

Carlo D'Ippoliti

Economists are still divided on the identification of the 'ultimate causes' of the euro crisis. Perhaps a mix of the two most diffused theses seems to be the most plausible explanation. On the one hand, the eurozone represents a failing attempt at sharing a common currency (the euro) without having a common governance of the economy. From this point of view, several economists note that the European Union (EU) federal budget is tiny in comparison to the task of managing aggregate demand; common bonds and mutualisation of public debts are off the table. Others question the strictly monetarist mandate of the European Central Bank (ECB), whose Statute prevents the ECB from buying European sovereign bonds and obliges it to only focus on the growth of consumer prices (although the interpretation of the Statute is controversial). On the other hand, a second explanation looks at the growing divergence of the European economies, in particular the sustained balance-of-payments imbalances that produced the accumulation of excessive foreign debt in the deficit countries (derogatorily called GIPSIs after the initials of Greece, Ireland, Portugal, Spain and Italy) and huge, possibly nonperforming, loans vis-à-vis the GIPSIs in the 'core' European countries (Germany, the Netherlands, Austria, Finland) (D'Ippoliti, 2012).

The political answer to the crisis so far has been made up of three ingredients:

1. a mildly expansionary monetary policy, which is restrictive compared to those of the Fed, the Bank of England or the Bank of Japan, and was mainly focused at providing liquidity to the stressed banks;
2. a restrictive fiscal policy, which produced such falls in GDP to actually increase the debt-to-GDP ratios of various GIPSIs;
3. 'structural reforms', i.e. supply-side measures aimed at reducing workers' bargaining power.

The rationale of this strategy is to force an adjustment of the deficit countries' balance-of-payments based on the immediate fall of their imports and then, through wage deflation, an increase of their exports.

The importance of non-price competitiveness

There are several grounds to criticise such strategy (the most obvious being Keynes's famous observation that surplus countries should contribute to balance-of-payments rebalancing). However, it seems convenient to focus here on a specific aspect and ask: how much should wages in Italy fall, in order for Fiat cars to be competitive with Volkswagen cars?

There is no answer of course. In the most industrialised countries such things as the kind and quality of the product or the way it is produced, i.e. 'non-price competitiveness', are normally more relevant in determining firms' performance than mere labour costs. Schumpeter used to write that price competition is like trying to enter a door by knocking on it, while the competitive adoption of new technology is like knocking with a bazooka.

The relevance of non-price competitiveness is indeed recognised by the current European establishment, for example in the 'Lisbon Agenda' or the Europe 2020 plans. Yet, the European way to 'recovery', as described above, only seeks to regain cost and price competitiveness on the side of the GIPSI countries. This is partly the consequence of a misleading reading of the data on wages and productivity, which concludes that wages in the GIPSIs grew too much, and it is thus fair now – and economically efficient – that workers pay the highest price of the crisis. The reason is that if wages grow more than average productivity, unit labour costs grow and price-competitiveness is reduced.

The ECB's position

Unfortunately, this approach is also present in a lecture given by Mario Draghi, ECB President, to the Euro Summit of 14 March 2013 (Draghi, 2013). Such presentation seems to have taken on a crucial role due to the historical time at which it came since – according to the *Frankfurter Allgemeine Zeitung* – it silenced the Eurozone leaders that were willing to challenge the austerity agenda.

The ECB has not replied to the accusation (Watt, 2013) of having 'massaged the data' by comparing a series expressed in nominal values (wages) with one expressed in real terms (productivity), with the result of visualising wages as inflating exorbitantly. However, even if this major mistake was not true, and both series were expressed in real terms (or both in nominal terms), at least three further remarks may impair Draghi's main argument, which was based on a series of misleading graphs.

Let us focus on slide 10, represented in Figure 7.1. There, the annual development of two variables from 1999 to 2013 is presented: 'productivity per employee' and 'compensation per employee'. The former measures the value of total output divided by the number of employed workers, the latter denotes total labour income divided by the same number of workers.[1] Thus, we have two variables that measure a monetary value and that could be expressed in euros (using the nominal exchange rate for the years before entry into force of the common currency). If we did so, we would obviously find that output per worker is higher than compensation per worker, because part of the value produced must cover firms' fixed costs and provide a profit. In the countries and periods considered in the slide, wages rarely exceed 60 per cent of productivity.[2] Yet, by looking at Mario Draghi's graphs, we

---

1. Presumably full-time equivalent workers, i.e. adjusting for differences in the average number of hours worked; otherwise one would incorrectly think that workers who work more are more 'productive'.

2. The figure is computed using the same AMECO database used in the presentation for reasons of comparability. For the same reason it refers to the total economy, although it would be more correct to exclude the public sector since construction productivity changes roughly equal labour cost changes.

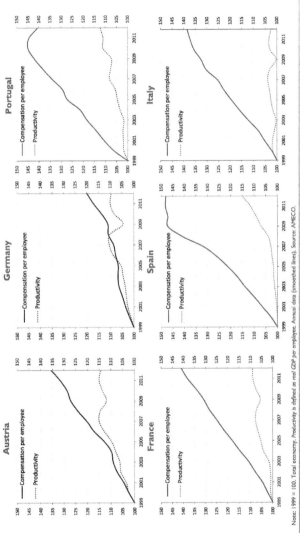

Figure 7.1 Slide 10 of Mario Draghi's Presentation at the March 2013 Euro Summit

get the impression that throughout Europe (even in Germany!) wages have become unbearably high, and we naturally come to agree with 'structural reforms', aimed at dragging down wages.

How did those graphs obtain such an odd result, showing wages remarkably higher than productivity, though they are not? Three technicalities should be noticed here.

1. Both variables are expressed with respect to a 'base year', i.e. they both take on value 100 in 1999. However, as we just saw, the two variables do not exhibit the same value in 1999. The reason for showing variables with respect to a base year is to highlight their *rate of growth*, instead of their value. So if Worker A earns 10 per cent of Worker B's wages, and if Worker A's wages double and while those of Worker B remain the same, Worker B still earns a lot more money than Worker A. In other words, rates of change provide useful information on the development of a variable through time, but they are frequently inadequate to compare two separate variables.[3] By contrast, this visualisation of the data magnifies the extent of the increase in unit costs.

2. Even if the point of the slide was to compare the rates of growth of the two variables, a second issue here is the time frame. Why do Draghi's graphs start from 1999, when the very database from which they are taken contains data from as far back as 1960? To focus on the impact of the euro is no adequate answer, because the entry into force of the common currency is only the last step of a decades-long process, through the European Monetary System, the Maastricht Treaty, the Amsterdam agreements, etc. If we look back to 1970s, we find that labour incomes have dramatically fallen as a share of GDP, precisely as a consequence of their lower growth with respect to average productivity.[4]

3. Finally, if we wanted to focus on just the last few years, it would still be useful to put the graphs into context. What cannot be seen from the slide is that nominal wages in several European countries grew more or less in line with prices, that is, the purchasing power of wages stayed

---

3. Thus, the slide shows that profits in the period considered tended to reduce as a proportion of wages, but from there we do not know anything concerning the aggregate value of profits.

4. One may argue that some rebalancing of the wage and profit shares may be welcome also in light of the interpretations of the crisis as produced, among other things, by growing income inequality.

constant. What was disappointingly lacking was productivity growth. Thus, the kind of policy intervention required to lower unit labour costs is productivity growth, not primarily a reduction of wages.

The EU as a neoliberal machine

Of course, one cannot say that Draghi's graphs or the slides are 'wrong', but certainly they exhibit a strong conservative bias. Given all this, one wonders how it is possible that during the presentation nobody in the eurozone ministers' staff noticed any of these shortcomings. It seems that the European leaders who are reluctant to pursue a strict austerity agenda may have a hard time coordinating a coherent alternative response, in the face of two centralised institutions (the ECB and the European Commission) pursuing a well-defined pro-austerity agenda with the crucial support of valuable research and data analysis facilities. There is, in a sense, a pro-austerity bias embodied in Europe's very institutional architecture, even abstracting from the actual content of its founding Treaties.

This is but one of the several in-built biases in the European architecture, that make it especially prone to unpopular policies and the neoliberal ideology. Another one, as Italy's experience suggests, is the *de facto* ban on second mandates. It may be sufficient to recall here Mario Monti's, the former Italian prime minister, political trajectory. After the sudden and welcome resignation of Silvio Berlusconi, Monti had been appointed head of government with the mandate to enact a strict pro-austerity 'technocratic' agenda. When the time for elections came, in desperate search for votes he suddenly had to become a pro-growth, skilled politician (Monti, 2013). Perhaps, if eurozone and EU leaders were to run for election, and if they were given the chance to be re-elected, they may feel more compelled to pursue growth-enhancing (and democratically legitimated) policies.

References

D'Ippoliti, C. (2012) 'There is more to Keynesianism than public spending alone', *PSL Quarterly Review*, Vol. 65, No. 260.

Draghi, D. (2013) 'Euro area economic situation and the foundations for growth'. Available from www.ecb.europa.eu.

Monti, M. (2013) 'Italy has led reform in Europe as well as at home', *Financial Times*, 21 January.

Watt, A. (2013) 'Mario Draghi's economic ideology revealed?' *Social Europe*, 26 March. Available from www.socialeurope.eu.

8

Europe's Lost Decade: Paths out of Stagnation

Hansjörg Herr

The Great Recession of 2008–10 reflects an economic instability that had built up over the previous decades. Within the European Monetary Union (EMU), the crisis of the financial market-driven development model is overlaid by a largely homemade state debt crisis and an undefined integration goal. The Western world, and more particularly Europe, is facing a lost decade.

The market radical globalisation project

The 1950s and 60s may be counted among the best years of the young capitalist social order. This was because everyone could have a slice of progress. The dynamic consumer demand was based on a relatively well-balanced income distribution. Investment activity was high and stable, given the low level of economic uncertainty and the stable development of demand. Precarious employment relationships were just as rare as complicated financial market products or obscenely high managerial pay. The 1970s saw the start of a crisis that reflected an inability to adapt the prevailing economic model. The crisis led, notably in the UK and the US, to the election of conservative governments who embarked on a radical reshaping of the policy framework.

Unstable financial markets

A shadow banking system developed, with new financial products and institutions based on high risks, short-termism and massively increasing debt of households, firms, governments and whole states. The central banks lost control over the money they were creating. The experience of recent decades has shown that far too great a share of credit went into speculative activity. The internet bubble of the 1990s was followed by an almost worldwide property bubble in the 2000s, together with other stock market or commodity bubbles. The deregulation of international capital movements left exchange rates to the whim of unstable international capital flows. Trade balances and international debt positions exploded, as did the number of currency crises and international financial market woes.

Over the past few decades, high indebtedness has built up a credit bubble that is now impairing development. Government debt has also increased dramatically. The rise in debt ratios has made the economic system more fragile, at a time when it is considerably less regulated than it was in the 1970s. If attempts to bring about a sustained growth process do not succeed, debt ratios will continue to rise even if hard consolidation efforts are made, and will further destabilise the system as a whole.

Market radical European integration

European integration also followed the logic of a market radical project. The institutionally insufficient integration led to low and partly negative real interest rates in some of the EMU countries, and stimulated real-estate bubbles. There was no strong fiscal centre in the EMU. The creation of a single currency, the euro, is a project which could also benefit workers by reducing interest rates, increasing potential GDP growth, supporting regions with development problems, and strengthening solidarity among countries. However, this potential has not materialised and the European project has turned into a nightmare for workers in many countries.

Deflationary risks

Precarious employment relationships and low-pay sectors have expanded, while trade union power has been eroded. Widening pay gaps and rising profit ratios have led to greater inequalities. From a macroeconomic point of view, uncontrolled market mechanisms within labour markets are highly dangerous. A wage development is functional if nominal wages rise in line with medium-term productivity trends in the overall economy plus the Central Bank's target inflation rate. In this case, nominal unit wage costs will rise at the same pace as the Central Bank's target inflation rate. This takes the pressure off monetary policy, as it will not be pushed into contractionary mode because of undesired inflationary wage increases, nor will it have to struggle against deflation due to falling nominal unit wage rates – a deflation that monetary policy would have difficulty in tackling.

Deflation increases the real debt burden and the financial system comes under pressure. Since the Great Depression of the 1930s, it has been clear that nominal wage reduction is a medicine that makes the patient worse: all the more so given the high debt positions also found in the private sector.

To seek a currency union without a political union is illusory. Without coordination of wage development, a currency area cannot be stable. Institutions are needed to guarantee coherent wage development within a currency union. In the EMU, wage coordination has failed. Nominal unit wage costs for the overall German economy stayed unchanged from 2000 to 2008, the last boom year, whereas in the Southern European countries over the same period they rose by 20 or even 30 per cent. Together with Germany's relatively low growth rate and hence relatively low imports, this led to large trade and current account disparities.

Growth in the later crisis countries was primarily generated by property bubbles. When they burst, domestic demand collapsed. Current account deficits further reduced demand. The fiscal policies required to stabilise plummeting demand and save the financial system led to rising public debt ratios. From 2010, in the eurozone doubts developed about the solvency and liquidity of governments in the crisis countries. The crisis countries are now in a jam: investment levels have hit rock bottom, current account deficits are reducing domestic growth, public budgets are under pressure to make savings and, given all of this, consumer demand is also weak.

The strategy for resolving the crisis of confidence in the solvency of Southern European public debts holds out little prospect of success. Public spending cuts and tax increases for the broad majority are further reducing demand and employment. One factor that is radically worsening the crisis is the forced reduction of nominal wages. This is leading to deflation and putting a heavy burden on the domestic financial system. Now not only governments in crisis countries have problems, but private debtors are also increasingly struggling to service their debt. In such a situation, there is no hope that the banking system in crisis countries can start to function again and extend credit to the private sector. The motivation for wage cuts in the crisis states is understandable, as it is aimed at reversing the previous, overly steep rise in unit wage costs. But a policy in the tradition of Chancellor Heinrich Brüning at the beginning of the 1930s will not work.

Policies needed to overcome the crisis

An immediate resolution of the public debt crisis in the EMU is feasible if the European Central Bank (ECB) guarantees the refinancing of public budgets within the EMU and, if necessary, purchases unlimited quantities of state bonds. It would then take on the role of lender of last resort also in regard to public debt, as do the central banks in the US, the UK and Japan. In addition, the rescue package aimed at stabilising the crisis countries needs to be expanded.

Interventions by the ECB or through the rescue package could be interpreted as an invitation to run irresponsibly high budget deficits. Institutional precautions must be taken to avoid such a moral hazard problem. Mario Draghi, president of the ECB, made it clear that the ECB would only support governments which would follow recommendations by the Troika (European Commission, International Monetary Fund and ECB). So there are no longer any obstacles to ECB interventions and expanded rescue packages.

In addition, a symmetrical stabilisation mechanism is needed in order to increase the surplus countries' imports. Surplus countries such as Germany must stimulate their domestic economies. This can be achieved through expansionary fiscal policies, as Germany does have some medium-term legroom, including for increased budget deficits. Advisable measures include taxing higher incomes and spending the revenue this would bring in. Thus, expansionary stimuli could be provided without running up debts.

Nominal wages must rise faster in the surplus countries than in the crisis countries. As nominal wage reductions should be avoided in the crisis countries because of their deflationary effects, wages in the surplus countries should be increased more strongly for several years. In this way, the imbalances within the EMU could be reduced in the medium term without courting the risks of deflation and inflation. Policymakers, especially in surplus countries like Germany, can and must back this goal by strengthening wage bargaining systems, introducing legal minimum wages and reducing precarious employment. Steps towards wage coordination within the EMU are also essential. Overall, the EMU's external trade is in balance. The ECB should pursue an exchange rate policy such that the trend is for the EMU's external trade to remain balanced.

As well as fiscal coordination of public budgets within the EMU, a stronger fiscal centre is also needed. This should receive part of the national tax revenues. It should be able to pursue an active counter-cyclical fiscal policy and to issue eurobonds with guarantees from all EMU countries. A stronger fiscal centre, up to and including an economic government, would increase the democracy deficit at the European level. To compensate for this, the role of the European Parliament must be strengthened.

Integration within the EMU must go hand in hand with a completely overhauled model of capitalism. Following the Great Recession, the market radical globalisation project seems to have had its day. What is needed is strict regulation of the financial markets, which should have a service function; a shift away from shareholder value as the guiding principle of enterprise management; a new regulation of labour markets; the achievement of balanced income distribution; a reform of global governance; and an ecological reorientation. In the current crisis, Europe is not an active partner for the development of the world economy in the direction mapped out here. Rather, it is a danger to the world economy. Things need not be that way.

References

Dullien, S., Herr, H. and C. Kellermann (2011) *Decent Capitalism: A Blueprint for Reforming our Economies* (London: Pluto Press).

Herr, H. and M. Kazandziska (2011) *Macroeconomic Policy Regimes in Western Industrial Countries* (London: Routledge).

9

The Crisis, Structural Reform and the Fortification of Neoliberalism in Europe

Christoph Hermann

Even though the crisis that erupted in 2008 was widely credited as failure of neoliberalism, the ensuing fiscal crisis presented an unexpected opportunity to fortify and deepen neoliberalism in Europe (Crouch, 2011). Essentially neoliberalism is a political ideology that claims that almost all social problems can be solved through market forces, even those that were created by the market in the first instance. A major outcome of the promotion of market forces is growing inequality. The new code word for neoliberal restructuring is structural reform. In those countries that are dependent on emergency loans from the European Stability Mechanism or from the International Monetary Fund, structural reforms were part of the economic adjustment programmes which the respective governments had to accept in exchange of the loans. Other countries had to accept similar reforms in exchange for the support of the European Central Bank, while again others adopted structural reforms as a precautionary measure to calm international creditors. Increasingly pressure for structural reforms is also built up through the European Semester and the country-specific recommendations issued by the European Commission on a yearly base to foster economic convergence (Hermann, 2014).

Structural reforms differ from regular austerity measures inasmuch as the goal is not primarily or not even to reduce public deficits; the main goal instead is to adapt the institutional framework of a given country in order to make it more competitive. Increased competitiveness in this view attracts investments and initiates growth. As the European Central Bank (2011: 7) notes, structural reforms 'help . . . countries to strengthen competitiveness, increase the flexibility of their economies and enhance their longer-term growth potential'. Preferred areas of reform include labour markets and collective bargaining systems. The Tables 9.1 and 9.2 summarise major structural reforms that were adopted in eleven EU member states during the crisis. The countries were selected on the ground that they were all strongly affected by the downturn.[5]

Table 9.1   Labour market reforms

Promotion of non-standard employment	
Promotion of fixed-term employment and agency work	EE, EL, LT, RO, PT
Introduction of new employment contracts with less pay and job security	EL ES
Extension of probation periods	ET, GR, RO
Reduction of job security	
Weakening of employment protection for civil servants	EL
Weakening of employment protection for particular vulnerable groups of employees	EE, HU, RO
Shortening of notice periods	EL, ES
Increasing thresholds and reducing obligations for mass layoffs	EE, EL, ES, RO
Changes in the definition of fair and unfair dismissals	ES, IT, UK
Reduction of severance pay	EE, ES, EL, PT
Restriction of access to court and reduction of fines for unfair dismissals	HU, UK
Elimination or weakening of the right to be reinstated after an unfair dismissal or after a mass layoff	ES, IT, RO

EE=Estonia, EL=Greece, ES=Spain, IE=Ireland, IT=Italy, LT=Lithuania, LV=Latvia, HU=Hungary, PT=Portugal, RO=Romania, UK=United Kingdom. Source: Own elaboration.

State sector employment

The state sector (especially state sector employment) is a popular site for financial consolidation and structural reform. The Greek government is aiming to reduce public employment by a third. The British government shed 420,000 jobs by 2012 and is well on course to reach its goal of cutting 10 per cent of the public sector workforce by the end of 2015. In countries we have analysed, most job cuts are planned in education and health care; while the UK simply dismisses public sector workers, other countries shrink the workforce primarily through the non-replacement of retirees, or through voluntary dismissals. After a temporary ban on new hiring, only every tenth state sector employee is meant to be replaced in Greece. In Romania this

---

5. The following sections are based on Hermann and Hinrichs 2012.

Table 9.2   Reform of collective bargaining

Decentralising collective bargaining	
Elimination or suspension of national collective agreements	IE, RO
Suspension of the favourability principle	EL, ES
Approval of exceptions and divergences	IT
Weakening of collective bargaining	
Suspension or reduction of extension procedures	EL, HU, PT, RO
Limitation of the 'after effect' of expired collective agreements	EE, EL, ES
Limitation of arbitration	EL
Interventions in collective bargaining	
Suspension of existing agreements	EL
Limitation of the duration of agreements	EL, RO
Weakening of trade unions	
Higher thresholds for representativeness of trade union organisations and abolishment of tripartite institutions	RO, HU
Promotion of alternative forms of employee representation at the cost of works councils and trade unions	EL, HU, PT

EE=Estonia, EL=Greece, ES=Spain, IE=Ireland, IT=Italy, LT=Lithuania, LV=Latvia, HU=Hungary, PT=Portugal, RO=Romania, UK=United Kingdom. Source: Own elaboration.

applies to every seventh and in Italy to every fifth worker who leaves the state sector. Job cuts are also frequently combined with wage cuts and pay freezes. Thus, while thousands of jobs were axed, Greece and Spain also increased working time for the remaining state sector workers.

While state sector reforms were accompanied by a reduction of public expenses, other reforms had no immediate effect on public finances. The aim of these reforms was, instead, to unleash a process of internal devaluation, which would supposedly increase the country's competitiveness, attract investments, create jobs and boost growth. In Greece and Ireland, internal devaluation included lowering the national minimum wage – in Greece by 22 per cent, and in Ireland by 12 per cent (in Ireland, the cut was reversed after a change in government). While cuts in minimum wages are an exception, a number of countries have introduced minimum wage freezes, and some, the possibility for companies to unilaterally cut wages for a limited period.

Labour markets

Labour markets are a popular target of structural reforms during the crisis and a number of countries have relaxed regulations on fixed-term employment. Greece and Spain have also introduced new employment contracts for younger (and in the case of Spain, unskilled) workers. These contracts extend for a period of two years and pay between 75–80 per cent of the national minimum wage. However, workers under these contracts do not only earn less, but they can also be laid off at any time, without being eligible for unemployment benefits. These workers can also be dismissed without reason during probation. Hence, some countries have extended the probation period, with the example of Greece extending it from two months to one year.

As part of the flexibility agenda, other changes have also made it easier to lay off workers. Special protection for vulnerable groups such as pregnant women, or workers on sick leave, have been relaxed, notice periods have been shortened, and severance pay has been cut back. Thus, new barriers have been introduced to struggles against unfair dismissals; and mass layoffs have been made easier (see Table 9.1).

Collective bargaining

There has been a dramatic change in collective bargaining systems, where various measures implemented enable a profound decentralisation, and an erosion of collective bargaining systems. These are indicated in Table 9.2.

Decentralisation has been imposed in three different ways: Firstly, countries have abandoned national or sector-wide collective agreements. Secondly, they have eradicated the 'favourability' principle, which stipulates that in the case of multiple collective agreements, the regulations that prevail are those that grant the most favourable conditions for the workers. With the suspension of this principle, employment and working conditions are now easily determined at company level. Thirdly, countries have promoted decentralisation through the granting of exceptions and exemptions, as well as the acceptance of deviations from sectoral standards.

Decentralisation is complemented by a weakening of bargaining institutions. A number of countries have suspended (or severely restricted) extension procedures through which agreements concluded by one (or more) employer organisations and unions are made binding for entire sectors or regions. Collective bargaining systems have also suffered from the elimination (or shortening) of the 'after effect' whereby regulations remain in force after agreements expire.

The crisis has also encouraged governments to interfere in collective bargaining in other ways. In Greece and Romania, new legislation limits the duration of collective agreements to three and two years respectively. In both cases, the International Labour Organisation has criticised the changes since they violate the principle of free bargaining. The erosion of the bargaining systems is complemented by a weakening of trade union representation. In Greece, for example, company agreements can now be negotiated by non-union affiliated staff representatives.

Structural reform and redistribution of wealth

As the previous paragraphs have shown, structural reforms include the reduction of state sector employment, the promotion of atypical employment and the reduction of job security, the decentralisation and weakening of collective bargaining, as well as the weakening of trade union representation. Hence with structural reforms competitiveness is increased at the cost of workers. Workers suffer from a lack of stable jobs, growing insecurity and from lower wages. However, the structural reforms in the crisis countries have so far failed to initiate a new phase of economic growth. Greece has suffered from six consecutive years of economic contraction and has lost almost 30 per cent of its pre-crisis GDP. Despite some signs of recovery, most countries covered in this analysis have still not made up for the losses incurred since the start of the crisis. However, while austerity and structural reforms have largely failed to boost growth they were very effective in redistributing wealth (Hermann, 2013). In five out of the eleven countries included in this analysis the gini coefficient, a measure of inequality, increased between 2008 and 2011. Ireland recorded the greatest proportional increase, followed by Spain and Hungary. The gap between the top and the bottom income quintile grew in six out of the eleven countries, signalling growing inequality among high- and low-income earners. Here the greatest increase was recorded in Spain, followed by Ireland and Italy. These figures may still underestimate the different exposure of different income groups to the crisis. A comparison between the development of disposable income of the top and bottom income decile shows that in six out of the eight countries from our sample for which data is available the top 10 per cent proportionally lost less income between 2007 and 2010 than the bottom 10 per cent – often half as much or less. Again Spain and Italy stand out in this comparison as here the top decile merely lost 1 per cent of disposable income, while the bottom decile lost 14 per cent in Spain and 6 per cent in Italy.

References

Crouch, C. (2011) *The Strange Non-Death of Neoliberalism* (London: Polity Press).

European Central Bank (2011) *Monthly Bulletin*, September.

Hermann, C. (2013) 'Crisis, structural reforms and the dismantling of the European Social Model(s)', *IPE Working Paper 26/13*, Berlin School of Economics and Law.

Hermann, C. (2014) 'Structural adjustment and neoliberal convergence in labour markets and welfare: The impact of the crisis and austerity measures on European economic and social models', *Competition & Change*, Vol. 18, No. 2.

Hermann, C. and Hinrichs, K. (2012) 'Die Finanzkrise und ihre Auswirkungen auf Sozialstaaten und Arbeitsbeziehungen – ein europäischer Rundblick', *Chamber of Labour*, Vienna. Available from www.arbeiterkammer.at.

10

The Economic Crisis and Job Quality in Europe: Some Worrying Trends and Worse May be to Come

Janine Leschke and Andrew Watt

The economic crisis has had a dramatic and lasting impact on labour markets worldwide. Seven years into the crisis the global labour market remains deeply scarred by the crisis, with the unemployment problem particularly severe in Europe.

But what have been the impacts on the *quality* of work? We can shed some light on this for the 27 member countries of the European Union using a Job Quality Index (JQI) developed at the European Trade Union Institute. We first calculated the JQI based on 2005 data. Our analysis showed wide dispersion across Europe with regard to job quality, with the Nordic countries but also the Netherlands and the UK performing best overall, while the Southern and most of the Central Eastern European countries were found in the other end of the spectrum. Using distinct sub-indices to cover various areas of job quality, the index however also showed that job quality is a multidimensional issue with important differences across countries, and also between the sexes (for detailed findings see Leschke et al., 2008). In 2012 we repeated the analysis based on 2010 data; by comparing the two sets of results we can see how job quality has changed on various dimensions over the five-year period and draw some conclusions about the impact of the first phase of the crisis. The full results are available in Leschke et al. (2012) and Leschke and Watt (2014); here we provide a brief analysis of the key findings.

Measuring job quality: key features of the ETUI's JQI

Whether one perceives one's job as being of high or low quality depends, obviously, on a mix of both subjective and objective factors. And the mix is complex: how can, for instance, a clean and safe working environment be weighed against, say, autonomy at work or the fact that one is working the 'right' number of hours? The interested reader will find a detailed description of the methodology underlying the JQI in Leschke et al. (2008). For the purposes of this article the following basic features need to be borne in mind.

The JQI divides job quality into six dimensions. They are:

1. the level and distribution of wages;
2. the (inverse of the) incidence of involuntary non-standard (that is fixed-term and part-time) work;
3. working-time and work-life balance issues;
4. physical working conditions, work intensity and autonomy;
5. the opportunity to acquire skills and develop one's career; and
6. workers' ability to represent their interests at work collectively.

Each of these areas is measured using a number of statistical indicators. As far as possible these are objective in nature. Numerous calculations were carried out to provide a score between 0 and 1 for each country on each of the six sub-indices. These are then averaged to produce the overall JQI. We can differentiate between men and women for all areas except collective interest representation.

The approach has some limitations. Note especially that we cannot say anything about the distribution of bad and good jobs *within* countries. In some areas data availability imposes constraints and makes value judgements inevitable. Still, the JQI does give us information on the way that job quality and some of its most important dimensions have changed in EU countries over a period in which labour markets have been shaken to their foundation by the crisis.

In particular we can test two opposing ideas. One is that as unemployment rises and workers' bargaining power falls, employers can impose bad working conditions on workers who have little option but to accept, resulting in worsening job quality (bargaining-power hypothesis). The other is that the crisis leads to the disproportionate shedding of low productivity 'bad jobs'; this so-called 'composition effect' would lead to a rise in average job quality.

The findings prove to be quite complex across different countries and job-quality dimensions. But at the risk of over-simplification – exceptions, caveats and a wealth of more specific information is available in the publications by the authors aforementioned – three key findings emerge.

Finding one: the crisis seems to have affected different dimensions of job quality in different ways

Figure 10.1 shows the results for the EU27 as a whole on the six job quality dimensions and for the overall JQI. Overall we see a decline in measured job quality, even if it is rather small. More interestingly we see quite substantial changes in four of the six components. But they go in different directions. The wages component declines appreciably, indicating that the purchasing power of wages for the average worker has fallen. Even stronger is the increase in the use of part-time and fixed-term contracts and/or in the extent to which workers reported that they were working in such jobs involuntarily. Moreover, the extent of workers who are afraid to lose their job has increased markedly. These are clear signs of the bargaining-power effect.

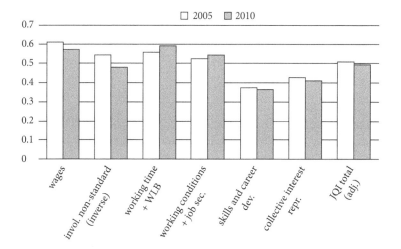

Figure 10.1   EU27 Job Quality Index results

On the other hand job quality has risen to the extent that excessive hours have been reduced and various measures of work intensity have improved. Also work autonomy seems to have improved. It seems likely that this is because jobs with low autonomy (for example in construction) have been disproportionately shed (composition effect).

The other two dimensions (skills development and collective interest representation) saw declines but of a rather small magnitude.

Finding two: job quality levels in Europe remain highly diverse

Figure 10.2 shows the overall JQI scores for the 27 EU member states in 2005 and 2010. The very substantial range across countries (from around 0.3 to 0.8 on our zero to one scale) has not changed in any major way, despite the fact that the worst performer in 2005, Poland, has seen the largest improvement. Apart from Poland, a rather mixed group of countries (headed by the Czech Republic, Belgium and Denmark) saw some rather minor improvements in measured overall job quality. The worst deteriorations were found in Ireland, France, the UK and Sweden.

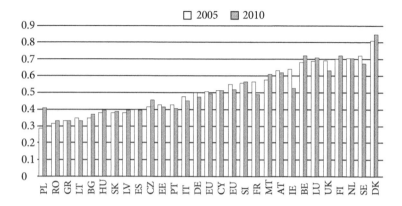

Figure 10.2   Overall JQI scores per country. NB: EU...=EU27 and EU15 respectively

These changes have not led to a major shift in the position of country groups known from the varieties of capitalism literature (such as the Nordic, Anglo-Saxon or 'southern' groups) in the distribution.

Finding three: there is a link between the severity of the crisis and overall job quality developments, but it is not particularly strong

Figure 10.3 plots the change in the unemployment rate between 2005 and 2010 against the change in the overall JQI over the same period. It must be noted that this also covers the pre-crisis period which in some countries was one of economic boom. The two extreme cases, Poland and Ireland, illustrate the fact that, respectively, an improving labour market situation in quantitative terms (i.e. falling unemployment) is associated with an improvement also in qualitative terms (higher JQI score), and vice versa. And there is a positive relationship across the whole distribution, although it is not particularly strong (Germany and Denmark, for instance, are at odds with this pattern). This is broadly in accordance with a bargaining-power explanation of job quality, but also technological and sectoral-change issues may well play a role (for a more in depth analysis from both an aggregate and individual level perspective refer to Erhel et al. (2012).

It is with respect to the incidence of involuntary part-time and fixed-term work, that the crisis link is most clear-cut. The countries with the most

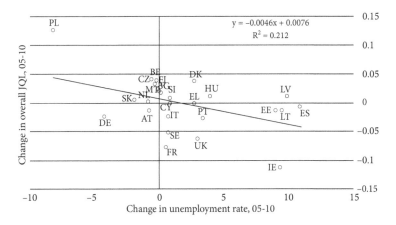

Figure 10.3   Change in unemployment rate versus change in overall JQI

serious deterioration include the UK and Ireland, the four crisis-hit southern EU countries and also Latvia and Hungary. On the other hand countries that showed a fall in the incidence of such forms of work included Poland, Belgium and Germany, where overall labour market trends were more favourable.

Some conclusions

The findings from our comparison of the JQI scores in 2005 and 2010 for the EU countries paint quite a complex picture. But it is clear that Europe's workers have been negatively affected not only by *quantitative* forms of labour market deterioration (lower employment, higher unemployment): on the whole they have also suffered a decline in the overall *quality* of their employment, at least as measured by our JQI and giving an equal weight to the six dimensions. If there are 'composition' effects – the destruction of low quality jobs – they are not sufficient to offset the loss of bargaining power which forces workers to accept lower quality jobs when there are fewer jobs to go around.

Even so, some elements of job quality have improved; workers have at least benefited from reduced work intensity in the crisis, and a lower incidence of excessive and unsocial working hours.

The data we analysed ended in 2010. It is likely that many of the effects of the crisis on job quality will take time to filter through. Moreover, in

Europe the crisis is far from over. This raises concerns about trends since 2010 and in the future. Alongside the more immediate and visible impact on the quantity of jobs, further studies – including more detailed qualitative studies that delve deeper than we can with the ETUI's aggregate approach – will need to monitor job quality, in its various dimensions, very closely in the coming years.

References

Erhel, C., Guergoat-Larivière, M., Leschke, J. and Watt, A. (2012) 'Trends in Job Quality during the Great Recession: a Comparative Approach for the EU', Available from: http://lnu.se.

International Labour Organisation (2014) 'Global Employment Trends', *International Labour Office*. Available from www.ilo.org.

Leschke, J. and Watt, A. (2008) *Job Quality in Europe*, Working Paper, (Brussels: ETUI). Available from www.etui.org.

Leschke, J. and Watt, A. (2014) 'Challenges in Constructing a Multi-dimensional European Job Quality Index', in: *Social Indicators Research*, Vol. 118, No. 1.

Leschke, J., Watt, A., with Finn, M. (2008) *Putting a number on job quality? Constructing a European Job Quality Index*, Working Paper (Brussels: ETUI). Available from www.etui.org.

Leschke, J., Watt, A. and Finn, M. (2012) *Job quality in the crisis – an update of the Job Quality Index (JQI)*, Working Paper (Brussels: ETUI). Available from www.etui.org.

SECTION 3

Exploring Alternatives

11

Tackling Unemployment and Growing Public Debt

Jomo Kwame Sundaram and Anis Chowdhury

In 2014 the IMF noted:

> The world economy is in the middle of a balancing act. On the one hand, countries must address the legacies of the global financial crisis, ranging from debt overhangs to high unemployment. On the other, they face a cloudy future. Potential growth rates are being revised downward, and these worsened prospects are in turn affecting confidence, demand, and growth today. (2014: xiii)

While global economic recovery remains anaemic, most industrialised countries continue to face growing unemployment and public debt. Average unemployment in the Organisation for Economic Co-operation and Development (OECD) countries rose from around 5 per cent in 2007 to over 8 per cent in 2012. The harmonised unemployment rate for the OECD countries remained stuck at over 7 per cent during 2013 and 2014.

The eurozone is faring worse, with unemployment over 11 per cent, and still rising in some countries. The unemployment rate in Spain rose to 26 per cent in 2012, with youth unemployment surging to 55 per cent. The overall unemployment rate in Spain remained over 25 per cent in 2014. In Greece, it stood at 27.2 per cent in January 2014, the highest in the European Union (EU), with youth unemployment edging towards 60 per cent. Total unemployment in the EU28 was 24.850 million in July 2014, with eurozone jobless totalling 18.4 million, the highest number since records began.

According to the International Monetary Fund (IMF), half the increase in youth unemployment in the eurozone was due to the decline in economic growth. In the most vulnerable eurozone economies – Cyprus, Greece,

Ireland, Portugal and Spain – lack of growth accounted for about 70 per cent of the rise in youth unemployment (Banerji et al., 2014).

When the crisis first hit, world leaders, including those in the largest economies of the G20, acted decisively, with large fiscal stimulus packages totalling about $2.6 trillion during 2008–10. The International Labour Organisation (ILO) estimated that 7 to 11 million jobs were created or saved in G20 countries by such stimulus packages in 2009. But with the emergence of supposed 'green shoots' of recovery from mid-2009, financial markets and media shifted attention to the ballooning public debt, especially in the eurozone, where countries borrow in euros, rather than in national currencies.

After the Great Recession hit developed countries in 2009, the public debt situation deteriorated rapidly. The average public debt in industrialised economies increased from around 70 per cent of GDP in 2007 to about 110 per cent in 2012. Most governments took drastic measures to curb government debt and deficits. Such drastic actions, it was claimed, would engender investor confidence and thus bring about economic recovery.

The fallacy of fiscal austerity

However, market confidence has not been restored. The advocates of this ostensible 'market confidence' view conveniently overlook the fact that when the austerity measures adversely affect growth, jobs, incomes and tax revenue, they reduce rather than raise market confidence.

The IMF has admitted that, together with many others, it had seriously underestimated multipliers, thus contributing to the depth of the resulting contractionary impact of austerity policies. The IMF also warned that: 'Frontloaded consolidations tend to be more contractionary and, hence, delay the reduction in the debt-to-GDP ratio relative to smoother consolidations' (Batini et al., 2012).

In fact, earlier IMF research had warned that 'slamming on the brakes too quickly will hurt the recovery and worsen job prospects. Hence the potential longer-run benefits of fiscal consolidation must be balanced against the short- and medium-run adverse impacts on growth and jobs' (Ball et al., 2011). Over the past three decades, fiscal consolidation has raised short- and especially long-term unemployment, hurting wage-earners disproportionately more than profit- and rent-earners. The IMF now also recognises that 'infrastructure investment, for example, even when financed by debt, may be justified and can help spur demand in the short term and supply in the medium term' (IMF 2014: xiv).

But IMF research seems to have little influence on its operations, policy advice and conditionalities. Hence, policymakers are still refusing to reconsider their approach to dealing with unemployment and debt. Instead, when the promised effects have not materialised, they have introduced yet more cuts, further choking economic recovery prospects.

New social compact

Austerity champions also believe that growth will come from a major expansion of export demand; but obviously, global economic recovery cannot be based on all countries finding external markets for their output. Hence, the response to growing unemployment and public debt has to focus on reinvigorating domestic demand, especially in developed economies.

This would entail both immediate policy actions to expand domestic demand as well as medium-term policies to address structural issues (such as infrastructure bottlenecks, which have been hampering productivity growth), and longer-term challenges such as climate change. This requires national consensus among government, business and workers.

The immediate task is to restore consumer and business confidence which depends on sales and profits prospects. This would require boosting spending which can be quickly achieved by reversing social protection and public employment cuts. Governments should expand public services, including active labour market programmes, subsidised childcare, universal healthcare and education. Such public provisioning enhances the 'social wage', taking pressure off wage demands as businesses strive to recover. These measures also help mitigate inequalities and enhance the welfare of all, thus contributing to social and political stability.

Such labour market policies typically come at modest fiscal cost. Increased spending on active labour market programmes costing 0.5 per cent of GDP can be expected to increase employment by between 0.2 and 1.2 per cent over the medium term by raising aggregate demand and better matching jobseekers with vacancies (ILO, 2012). Moreover, well-designed unemployment benefits and active labour market programmes not only provide much-needed income support, but also prevent skill erosion by keeping workers employed and providing training.

As the government fulfils its side of the bargain, there will be fewer wage demands not supported by productivity gains. This will not only remove the need for contractionary monetary policy to contain inflationary pressure, but also lower borrowing costs for investors. As restrained wage demands and borrowing costs help repair the balance sheets of businesses, investors must be induced by appropriate measures to invest in the real economy, instead of financial speculation.

Global Green New Deal

Almost eight decades ago, President Franklin Roosevelt introduced the New Deal for a strong and sustained economic recovery. Not only did it lift the United States out of the Great Depression, but it also addressed unsustainable agricultural practices that had caused widespread environmental, economic and social distress, and helped usher in a new era of economic growth and prosperity, especially in some poorer regions.

The current crisis also needs a New Deal-type response, but after decades of globalisation and environmental deterioration, it must also involve international cooperation and coordination as well as a collective global commitment to sustainable development. The current crises are global in nature, and appropriate and adequate responses are needed in all countries.

Such a Global Green New Deal (GGND) would have elements including public works programmes in line with the Global Jobs Pact and support for social protection contributing to a Global Social Protection Floor. The GGND should, therefore, be central to the broader international counter-cyclical response to the crisis complemented by national stimulus packages in all countries aimed at reviving and greening national economies.

Back to public debt?

The GGND will inevitably increase public debt in the near term; but this should not pose a longer-term problem as it will engender sustained economic growth and employment recovery – as the New Deal did eight decades ago.

Many countries had huge public debts when the Second World War ended. Despite similar calls then for drastic expenditure cuts, governments spent a great deal more on economic reconstruction and social protection measures. If they had caved in to the fiscal hawks of their time, post-war European recovery would have been delayed and the Cold War would have been lost at the outset.

As governments continued with massive expenditure to rebuild their countries, economies grew all over the world, and debt burdens diminished quickly with rapid economic growth and fast growing tax revenues. These experiences show that deficits and surpluses should be adjusted counter-cyclically over the course of business cycles rather than, say, annually.[1]

There is, of course, one big difference between then and now. The financial sector is much more powerful now, with governments often held hostage by financial markets and the whims of rating agencies. The record of rating agencies before the 2008 global economic crisis is now widely recognised as abysmal, with even the US Congress seriously debating whether they should be prosecuted.

To make matters worse, there is still no agreed procedure for sovereign debt work-outs.[2] The protracted difficulties in resolving the Greek crisis underscore the urgent need for a fair and orderly sovereign debt work-out mechanism for all countries.

Concluding Remarks

Harsh fiscal measures, without offsetting efforts to foster growth and job creation, typically fail to induce growth, create jobs, raise incomes and restore investor confidence. Instead, they exacerbate unemployment and social unrest, and are politically unsustainable.

---

1. The five cyclical stages of fluctuating levels of economic activity that an economy typically experiences are: growth (expansion), peak, recession (contraction), trough and recovery.

2. The process of working out a satisfactory method to enable a debtor country to recover or grow in order to repay external debt, typically involving restructuring, adjustment and provision of new finance.

A better way out is by deepening tripartite social dialogue among investors/employers, employees and governments. Only genuine social dialogues can reconcile competing demands on meagre resources as all parties can clearly see and address the costs and benefits as well as trade-offs among various difficult policy options.

References

Ball, L., Leigh, D. and Loungani, P. (2011) 'Painful medicine'. *Finance & Development*, September.

Banerji, A., Saksonovs, S., Lin, H. and Blavy, R. (2014) 'Youth Unemployment in Advanced Economies in Europe: Searching for Solutions', IMF Staff Discussion Note SDN/14/11.

Batini, N., Callegari, G. and Melina, G. (2012) 'Successful Austerity in the United States, Europe and Japan'. IMF Working Paper WP/12/190.

ILO (2012) *Global Employment Outlook* (International Labour Organisation: Geneva).

IMF (2014) *World Economic Outlook* (International Monetary Fund: Washington: DC).

12

Tax for Equity (T4E): Getting Wages Back on Track[3]

Frank Hoffer

During the last few decades productivity gains have not been shared fairly in most societies. The resulting growth in inequality has been one of the root causes of the crisis. Austerity and further aggressive wage cuts are

---

3. I would like to thank Patrick Belser, Janine Berg, Eckhard Hein, Pierre Laliberté, Sangheon Lee, Nicolas Pons-Vignon, Achim Truger and Lesley Walker for their comments on an earlier draft.

currently aggravating the problem. As wage developments are continuously trailing long-term productivity growth, governments need to act in leading economies back to a more balanced growth path. Profits generated by monopolising productivity gains and depriving workers of wage rises in line with productivity should become subject to special taxation. Such a Tax for Equity (T4E) would ensure fair competition and close the opportunity for profit maximisation through wage repression.

Sharing productivity growth

To ensure inclusive and sustainable growth, productivity gains have to be shared between capital and labour. For this to happen, real wage growth needs at least to match the long term productivity growth in a society. As central banks aim at a certain level of inflation, nominal wage growth needs therefore to equal national productivity growth plus the targeted inflation rate of the Central Bank. Following such a balanced wage norm the increased productive capacity will be absorbed by the higher aggregate demand resulting from the simultaneous increase of wages and profits. Wage growth below productivity leads to either deflation as witnessed in Japan or aggressive export surplus strategies as in Germany; or – if prices are sticky – a decline in real wages, aggregate demand, production and employment. As markets have failed to deliver such balanced wage developments there is a need for policy intervention to stop the macro-economically undesirable wage repression. Wage restraint was achieved in many countries through a weakening of the collective bargaining system, an unprecedented rise in precarious employment and the creation of large unprotected low pay sectors.

Towards rational wage setting

Trade unions are too weak to ensure a fair-sharing of productivity gains, and decisions by governments to enlarge the legal scope for unprotected forms of work have made things worse. The insufficient wage growth has resulted in a global lack of aggregate demand. To avoid further deflationary downward pressure on wages, and beggar-thy-neighbour policies, requires that enterprises do not abuse their market position and do not force desperate workers to accept low wages. There is a need to correct the power imbalance in the labour market that results in ever greater inequality and dysfunctional macroeconomic outcomes. With depressed wages, even higher profits do not result in increased investment, because investment decisions are not so much based on past profits than on future profit expectations.

Current wage-setting practices allow unproductive enterprises to stay afloat by receiving *de facto* wage subsidies from the workers. This has the same negative impact on overall productivity as other subsidies that artificially maintain uncompetitive enterprises in the market. From the enterprise perspective there is no difference whether the subsidy is a government hand-out or a wage concession. As with other subsidies, wage concessions might be justified as an emergency measure to absorb an economic shock, but they should never be permanent.

In light of the failure to maintain decent wage growth, there is a need for policy to reverse this socially and economically negative trend. Governments should support systems of more centralised or coordinated wage-setting. An efficient way would be taxation that makes it unattractive for enterprises to push wages below the productivity-related wage norm. Any cost savings gained from lower nominal unit labour costs achieved by undercutting the wage norm should be highly taxed.

Taxing wage dumping

How would this work? Every enterprise would report the hourly wage of their employees to the tax authorities. The difference between the average hourly wage increase actually paid to all employees except executive management and the wage norm will be subject to the tax for equity (T4E).

With the T4E, companies underpaying their employees – meaning paying a wage increase below the wage norm – would have to pay a 75 per cent tax on cost savings achieved through underpaying workers. The rate should not be set at 100 per cent, as there might be situations that justify a slight deviation from the wage norm. The T4E gives a strong incentive for workers and employers to share prosperity and it can be assumed that it will support collective bargaining processes. Employers will most likely prefer to give a motivating pay rise to their workers instead of paying higher taxes and as a one-dollar reduction in wages will only result in 25 cents of cost savings, the economic case for wage repression is much weaker. Workers will also feel more confident in demanding fair wages as this is supported by state tax policies. Under these new rules of the game, only in extremely difficult economic situations would wage agreements below the wage norm be expected. The high tax rate would only be imposed on cost savings that have been gained by underpaying the employees. Hence, it will only create an additional 'tax burden' for enterprises that achieve a business advantage through unfair labour practices. The tax would not replace collective bargaining as a wage-fixing mechanism. Employers can freely choose to share the productivity gains with their employees through adequate wages, or with society at large through the T4E. However, their ability to gain a competitive advantage by wage subsidises from their workers would be severely limited. But would employers not try to circumvent the tax through further outsourcing? There is no tax that business is not trying to circumvent, but as the tax would apply for all employers including employment agencies it would not create an additional incentive for outsourcing.

The tax would improve the competitive position of highly productive enterprises that share their productivity gains with their employees. The T4E would strengthen the market position of the best enterprises economically and socially and allow them to grow faster as they would no longer suffer from unfair competition through wage dumping. It would massively decrease incentives for employers to abuse market power. The tax would speed up structural change and force unproductive enterprises to exit the market. As rapid productivity growth is the best guarantee for increased prosperity, that is intended and in principle desirable. However there might be short-term restructuring needs that make it difficult to meet the wage norm in a specific year. Therefore, enterprises should be able to claim an exemption for a maximum of two years within a decade, if this request is agreed with the workers' representatives or, in its absence, by a two-thirds majority of the workforce.

Can it work?

But wouldn't the T4E price people out of work? Within the dominant economic discourse the explanation for poverty wages is low marginal productivity of the worker, and the reason for unemployment is wages above the market clearing level. Any increase in labour costs above the market level will benefit some by pricing others out of employment. However, the current crisis where millions of highly skilled people can't find work at any wage shows how wrong this mantra of neoclassical economists is. It implies that the level of employment is determined in the labour market, while in the real world it depends on the level of aggregate demand. The latter is determined by investment + consumption + exports − imports. Supporters of unprotected labour markets have so far failed to provide conclusive evidence that lower wages, or higher wage dispersion, have resulted in better employment performance. Ultimately, employment generation through wage repression only works if it increases international competitiveness and generates export surpluses. However, competitiveness is a relative term and one country can only gain competitiveness, if another one loses and as planet earth is a closed economy and not all countries can sell more than they buy.

Isn't T4E merely a nice idea, impossible to implement in the age of globalisation? Not at all. Globalisation has no direct impact on wages in non-tradable sectors where, in many countries, the most dismal wage developments have been observed. Concerning the export sector, it would obviously be desirable that no country aims at a constant trade surplus. It would be optimal if, after readjusting current imbalances, all countries would follow productivity-oriented wage policies at the aggregate level. However, in the absence of international coordination adjustments in the exchange rate, or where that proves to be impossible, a strategic use of Value Added Tax (VAT) would allow countries to pursue a productivity-orientated and equitable wage policy. Governments can always, in a revenue-neutral way, increase VAT, and lower non-wage employment costs. Exports would become more competitive, and the relative prices of imports would increase. Both factors would help to counter unfair trading practices based on wage repression.

Slashing wages and squeezing the poor is not only morally bad, it is just not working as a way out of the crisis. As the old recipes are failing we certainly do not need more of the same. T4E offers the opportunity to rebalance our economies and our societies by penalising wage dumping, rewarding the most competitive enterprise and, ensuring fair wages.

13

The State as the Employer of Last Resort

Cédric Durand and Dany Lang

The Great Recession the rich economies entered in 2007 has turned into social devastation in Europe. In France, there is every reason to despair of the new rulers holding the reins since June 2012. Policies implemented by François Hollande's government include budgetary austerity on a scale unprecedented since the Second World War (€60 billion worth of cuts planned over five years), the institutionalising of the European 'golden rule' which limits structural deficits to 0.5 per cent of GDP, a 'competitiveness' plan and a 'responsibility' pact which offers firms €50 billion in tax credits (€7 billion of which are to be funded by a VAT increase) and reduction of taxes and social contributions without any counterpart, and the transposition into law of an agreement reached between employers' organisations and minority trade unions aimed at increasing dramatically external number flexibility on the 'labour market'. The final step launched in the autumn of 2014 is an all-out liberalisation of the economy, which includes a lighter regulation of work on Sundays, some privatisations and the opening to market competition of several regulated professions and sectors. This profoundly neoliberal orientation is based on choices that need to be analysed.

The first is austerity. The deflationary exit strategy from the crisis advocated by the European elites can only lead to a long, painful recession. In the wake of a financial crisis, the private sector needs to get out of debt. If, in addition, the state takes to cutting back its expenditure, the spiral of depression can only get worse (Koo, 2011). For four years, the forecasts made by the Troika (European Commission, IMF and ECB) have been systematically contradicted by the facts, precisely because of their refusal to contemplate this basic macroeconomic mechanism. Indeed, a recent IMF study admits as much (Blanchard & Leigh, 2013). While the IMF used to think that a €1 cut in public spending reduces GDP by only €0.5, it has realised that, in fact, it leads to a contraction of activity representing between €0.9 and €1.7.

So while austerity is spreading across Europe, there is not the slightest chance of keeping Hollande's promises about turning the unemployment curve back down again in 2013. And yet, there is nothing 'natural' about the scourge of unemployment.

The limits of an investment revival

Hyman Minsky is the most feted economist since the financial crisis. Since August 2007, the *Wall Street Journal* (Lahart, 2007) has been a cheerleader for this posthumous glorification. On the fringes of academia, Minsky had explained that finance generates violent, destabilising cycles. One of the first formulations of his *financial instability hypothesis* is to be found in an article published in 1973, 'The Strategy of Economic Policy and Income Distribution' (Minsky, 1973). Here, Minsky identifies two anti-unemployment strategies that are richly instructive today. Under the first one, there is a 'view that economic growth is desirable, and that the growth rate is determined by the pace of private investment'. This leads to 'the emphasis on private investment as the preferred way to achieve full employment'. So the aim of the recovery policy is to ensure that investors' profit expectations turn back upwards, thus enabling accumulation to restart.

This involves tax deductions on investments as well as public procurement (typically, armaments or construction and public works) and subsidies for the construction sector or R&D. He sees numerous weaknesses in this strategy: it leads to a rise in capital's share of overall income, it nurtures unstable financial relations, it contributes to an increase in wage inequality and the spread of consumerism, and it can also cause inflation. Today, it should be added that these policies are coming up against the limits of capitalist growth. The exhaustion of industrial dynamics in the rich countries, the increased demand for services produced by people for people (health, leisure, education etc.) and the declining environmental conditions come at a time when the century-old trend towards slower productivity growth demands a fundamental rethink of what the industrial dynamics may be in future (Gordon, 2012).

Fitting public jobs to unemployed capabilities

The anti-unemployment strategy preferred by Minsky focuses on public employment. Its central principle is that of the state as the 'employer of last resort' (ELR). Under this approach, now advocated notably by the Modern Monetary Theory (MMT) economists, the state – or local authorities – pledges to provide employment to all those who are prepared to work at the basic public sector wage rate (and possibly above that rate, depending on the qualifications required for the jobs offered).

This 'takes the unemployed as they are and fits public jobs to their capabilities', but it is not *workfare*. Making jobs available does not imply an obligation to work; it does not replace, but rather supplements, the existing unemployment benefit and social assistance schemes. The jobs are in labour-intensive services which generate useful effects that are immediately apparent to the community in fields such as assistance to older people, children and the sick, urban improvements (green spaces, social mediation, restoration of buildings etc.), the environment, school activities, art initiatives and so on. A characteristic of all these activities is that they take place in sectors where the scope for productivity gains is weak or non-existent. As Minsky put it, the aim is 'better application of current capabilities' rather than increasing them.

Girding for a fiscal confrontation with capital

Strongly redistributive taxation and the savings made on unemployment benefits would provide the means of paying for these jobs. Such a strategy would also lead to 'a rather quick partial euthanasia of the rentier'.[4] Indeed, there is 'no need to stimulate investment [. . .] Thus, truly progressive and effective death duties can be instituted'. And taxes on profits 'no longer need be determined by a need to sustain corporated cash flows'. This is especially so since for more than three decades, most profits have not been reinvested (Stockhammer, 2007) but distributed to the shareholders. Another advantage is that, unlike an indiscriminate revival policy, this policy of public ELR is directly targeted towards the unemployed, who are not only most in need of it but also constitute unused production capacity.

---

4. All the quotes in this paragraph are from Minsky (1973).

Given the immense human and social waste represented by unemployment, what is stopping governments from adopting such a policy? The answer is that the 'competitiveness' agenda is the one preferred by business. If focused on costs, the 'competitiveness' strategy aims, by lowering the wages or taxes paid by firms, to revive investment and employment through higher profitability and greater market share. If focused on moving upmarket, it entails mobilising public expenditure to support innovation and training, as ways of improving productivity. In either case, the reasoning depends on the possibilities for capital appreciation in a highly competitive context – which implies that, to a great extent, the hoped-for benefits of these policies will be to the detriment of trading partners.

On the other hand, the ELR strategy points the available labour towards social needs. It aims to produce use value. Combined with other ambitious policies, such as a major investment programme for environmental conversion, it would enable the disbandment of the 'reserve army' of unemployed people and the reduction of inequalities by shifting the income distribution more towards wages. It is thus clearly unfavourable towards the holders of capital, particularly the rentiers.

However, putting an ELR strategy into practice does mean changing the framework for integration in the world economy and, more immediately, for European integration. Defensively, there is a need to prevent the capital flight that would inevitably be triggered by a resolute tax policy (if necessary, by recourse to currency controls) and to stabilise imports, either through exchange rate depreciation policies or through quota measures.

On the offensive side, a public debt financing system should be put in place backed by household savings in the countries that jointly agree to apply this policy, while requiring the Central Bank to guarantee the securities issued. There is also a need to lift the curbs that free trade places on the possibilities for orientating economic activity towards the production of use value and the preservation of the biosphere. This entails taking measures that promote the shortening of production circuits and negotiating agreements to stabilise prices in the medium term, particularly for raw materials and foodstuffs.

If such measures sound radical, they are nothing compared to the market fanaticism that has now taken hold of our political leaders. This fanaticism leads them to reject out of hand options that would enable unemployment and inequality to be vigorously tackled. Isn't that the kind of daring that might be expected from a straightforwardly left-wing policy?

References

Blanchard, O. and Leigh, D. (2013) 'Growth Forecast Errors and Fiscal Multipliers', IMF Working Paper, WP/13/1. Available from www.imf.org.

Gordon, R.J. (2012) 'Is U.S. Economic Growth Over? Faltering Innovation Confronts the Six Headwinds', NBER Working Paper, No. 18315. Available from www.nber.org.

Koo, R.C. (2011) 'The world in balance sheet recession: causes, cure, and politics', *Real-World Economics Review*, issue no. 58. Available from www.paecon.net.

Lahart, J. (2007) 'In Time of Tumult, Obscure Economist Gains Currency', *Wall Street Journal*, 18 August.

Minsky, H.P. (1973) 'The Strategy of Economic Policy and Income Distribution' (1973). Hyman P. Minsky Archive. Paper 353. Available from http://digitalcommons.bard.edu.

Stockhammer, E. (2007) 'Some Stylized Facts on the Finance-Dominated Accumulation Regime', Working Papers 142, Political Economy Research Institute, University of Massachusetts at Amherst. Available from www.peri.umass.edu.

14

'We are Steaming Ahead': NUMSA's Road to the Left[5]

An Interview with Karl Cloete

The expulsion of the National Union of Metal Workers of South Africa (NUMSA) from the Congress of South African Trade Unions (COSATU) in November 2014 was a watershed moment. It deepened further the crisis in the Alliance between the ANC, COSATU and the South African Communist Party (SACP). In addition to fighting for a radical shift amongst trade unions, NUMSA also played a major role in the establishment of a new United Front which will be launched in 2015.

---

5. This is an edited version of an interview published in full in *The Bullet* in March 2015.

In December 2014 Sam Ashman (SA) and Nicolas Pons-Vignon (NPV) interviewed Karl Cloete (KC) about a tumultuous year and the road ahead.

SA / NPV: Those who are not in South Africa may think that NUMSA is responsible for undermining COSATU and working class unity. How would you respond to this?

KC: When COSATU was established in 1985, NUMSA was in the centre of the unity talks. COSATU was a product of collective struggle and the federation shook the South African landscape under apartheid and played an important part in the 1994 democratic breakthrough. But COSATU, particularly over the last eight years, has almost totally shed its independence. It has become embroiled in factional politics within the ANC and the SACP. The COSATU that used to be a campaigning formation has become an organisation unable to take forward critical struggles – around precarious work, unemployment, the privatisation and commodification of services. We are challenging legally our expulsion and we have appealed for the convening of a COSATU Special National Congress (SNC). COSATU's history is not something you walk away from easily.

SA / NPV: How has COSATU got into such a situation, given this history?

KC: Today COSATU is limited to forming part of the ANC's election machinery. Beyond that, it has been a real struggle to influence policy. That has been the case over the last 20 years, since what happened to the Reconstruction and Development Programme (RDP).[6] It was a COSATU sponsored idea which originated within NUMSA. We felt the new government should do certain things to reconstruct our country, to move away from white minority rule at the expense of the black majority and to have redistributive policies to address the skewed ownership and control of the economy. The RDP became a compromise between the alliance partners but even after the compromises the RDP office in the government was closed down, without consultation. A new economic framework was introduced in 1996 and since then the ANC government has followed a neoliberal path. Today the National Development Plan follows exactly the same pattern. COSATU is a mere rubber stamp for neoliberal policies. It is

---

6. The ANC election manifesto in 1994.

useful for the ANC government to have a labour federation allied to itself, but one which will not make too many noises.

Secondly, there is the old question of wearing too many hats. You have several members of the Central Executive Committee who have multiple leadership roles. The President of COSATU is also a member of the SACP Central Committee, a member of the SACP Politburo, and a member of the ANC's National Executive Committee. So COSATU can today take a position, but then you leave COSATU and you go and sit in the ANC NEC, and you are persuaded differently. And what happens invariably is that you compromise COSATU's position.

The third problem is that the ANC and the SACP have started to say to COSATU that its outlook has become 'oppositionist', that we speak a language which is anti-ANC and anti-Alliance, and that as a trade union movement we have become 'too political'. That contestation has become factionalised – with one faction supporting the status quo coming from the ANC and SACP, and the other faction saying that our loyalty is to the membership, and to our resolutions, campaigns and programmes.

SA / NPV: Do you think the unity of COSATU still can be saved? Or has the time come for NUMSA, and the unions supporting it, to build a new independent federation?

KC: A couple of things need to be mentioned here. Firstly the dominant faction within the 'voice of reason' brigade is constituted by the public sector unions. That is interesting for a number of reasons. In June 2013 at the SACP 13th National Congress there was a paper delivered that called for a different way of organising in the public sector, along the lines of 'take responsibility for the revolution' – i.e. unions must not be in opposition to government programmes. They must be for better public service delivery, even if it is under austerity measures. So your role must be different to those in the industrial sectors or mining. And that perspective plays itself out within COSATU and it relates to my earlier point about the president of COSATU being a senior member of the SACP. A divide has developed between private sector unions like NUMSA and the public sector unions where there is no tolerance of dissent. This has brought many in the public sector to realise that the leaders have turned against their own constitutions and members. Democratic practices are thrown out of the window. People have decided it is time to challenge the dominance of a conservative, right-wing and corrupt leadership in these unions who behave as though they are shop stewards of the ANC and the SACP.

This is the reason behind the call for the formation of a new public sector union. This has nothing to do with NUMSA, it would be wrong for us to call for this, but I do think that people were inspired by the resolutions taken at the December 2013 NUMSA Special Congress.

In COSATU at the moment you have eight other unions against the NUMSA expulsion. They decided to demand the unconditional reinstatement of NUMSA back into COSATU and said they will not participate in any of COSATU's structures unless that happens. COSATU's President says over and over again that NUMSA is expelled but metal workers must remain within the federation; some have gone to the extent of building a rival to NUMSA that has applied for membership.

We decided to go to court to expose the deliberate project to get NUMSA expelled and because we want to ensure there is respect for the rules of the federation. NUMSA's view is to fight to reclaim COSATU even if you need to use the courts, but if all else fails we must begin the process of building a new labour federation. It is painful, when you give birth to something and you are no longer a part of it, but you have to move on. The reality is that only 30% of workers in South Africa are organised into unions.

SA / NPV: Why do you see a need to return to the mass democratic politics of the 1980s, and how do you see the United Front going forward?

KC: South Africa is the service delivery protest capital in the world; the neoliberal policies imposed on our people are resisted, but that is a leaderless resistance. It has no direction. Sometimes the protests get violent and the anger is not properly directed. We need a new United Front [after the United Democratic Front of the 1980s] to bring together workplace and community struggles.

One day the SACP says that NUMSA is a 'workerist' formation, the next day they say we are too political, go back to the workplace. But we have always believed in community and workplace struggles coming together. We should bring communities into worker action and worker action into communities. This is a re-awakening; we have got to take our power back. We have been hijacked by a small, black elite who feast on the state through corrupt means. If we don't get onto the streets, we are not likely to change things.

SA / NPV: We have already seen an aggressive response to developments in NUMSA. Phones have been tapped, cars and offices broken into, and three shop stewards were murdered in 2014. How do you plan to take on this very clear opposition?

KC: It will never be easy to build an alternative to the ANC, a 103-year-old national liberation movement. In Africa and Third World countries you find huge sentimental attachment to the party that liberated the people. We have no illusions that it will be hard work. But it is necessary work politically to get people to regain confidence. Many who have remained loyal to the ANC this time around decided not to vote. If you hone into some of the metros [large municipalities], the ANC has lost its grip. This is what we must discuss at the launch of the United Front: are we ready to field candidates for local government elections in 2016, and on what platform, or would a Workers' Party have to contest elections?

SA / NPV: How do you see NUMSA going forward as a trade union of metal workers? How far should NUMSA try to steer all these different struggles?

KC: NUMSA will remain a trade union and not transform into a political party. We see de-industrialisation and we think there is no better time to re-industrialise. Beneficiation [of mineral resources] is all talk but there is no action. NUMSA has a task. We have bargaining in all the metal and engineering sectors and autos. We have a plan up to our national congress in 2016 that requires internal union work to service the membership but also to speak to broader socio-economic issues.

On all fronts an alternative is necessary, but NUMSA must never change the foundation on which it rests – fighting oppression, discrimination and exploitation wherever it is in society and ensuring working-class control in the economy, dealing with gender inequality, taking up shop floor issues. NUMSA is probably the only growing union in South Africa. We said in 2012 that by 2016 we ought to be 400,000 and we are getting closer. In July 2014 we had 346,000 members. You can't feed workers with political slogans. This is why we insist that being a union, responding to the needs of workers, is central and non-negotiable.

SA / NPV: How do you situate NUMSA in relation to other international attempts to resist neo-liberalism?

KC: We do international work on the basis of respect for others' independence and political views, and their respect for ours, but realising we are fighting a common enemy. We have links with many countries. In Brazil, we have relationships with the MST and CONLUTAS, but we are not walking away from CUT [Central Única dos Trabalhadores – Unified Workers' Central, the main national trade union centre in Brazil] or PT [Partido dos Trabalhadores, or Workers' Party]. Old friends and new friends must appreciate that we will work with anyone who shares our perspective. We are not going to shed our relationship with IG Metall in Germany but we are making new friends in Die Linke. We are working with comrades in Bolivia and excited about the return of Morales; in the US we have many connections, and we recently received a big delegation from UNITE in the UK. In particular countries there may be tensions; we will not interfere but nobody must choose for us who we will work with. We are doing an international study tour as part of exploring the new Movement for Socialism; and will be convening a national conference on socialism. We are steaming ahead.

15

Alternatives to Neoliberalism: Towards a New Progressive Consensus

João Antônio Felício

In its *Working for the Few* briefing paper, Oxfam has called attention to a worrying trend: the wealth of 1 per cent of the world's richest people is equivalent to a total of US$ 110 trillion – 65 times the total wealth of the poorer half of the world's population.[7] In the last 25 years, wealth has been increasingly concentrated in the hands of a few; leading to a tiny elite owning 46 per cent of the world's wealth. An aggravating factor in this situation is

---

7. Available from www.oxfam.org.

that this wealth is mostly from profits derived from capital, property and assets, rather than from wages, as French economist Thomas Piketty recently showed in his outstanding book, *Capital in the Twenty-First Century*. A large number of highly profitable businesses are often under-taxed – an unacceptable trend across stock markets around the world. Ultimately, this contributes to economic inequality and creates a new *Belle Époque*, in which the social mobility of the working class is severely limited by the system of 'patrimonial capitalism'.

The price of inequality

The growth of inequality has serious consequences. As well as being questionable from a moral standpoint; it has serious economic consequences: inequality reduces consumers' purchasing power and demand, putting limits on the sustainable economic growth encouraged by the domestic market and compromising poverty reduction. Furthermore, the perpetuation of inequality in today's capitalism, where the upper class controls the economy in an almost hereditary fashion, ends up establishing a glass ceiling that makes the social mobility of the less favoured classes impossible. Piketty unmasks a recurring statement in conservative discourse: the differences in income are justified by the merit of exceptionally talented individuals who lead large companies (super managers).

On the contrary, Piketty shows that companies are controlled by family dynasties, they are empires handed down from father to son, often regardless of talent and merit (or work!).[8] This situation causes a sense of profound injustice for those who work hard without managing to significantly improve their wages, while having to witness dismissals and cuts in benefits because of 'difficult circumstances', and watching the managers at the top go to work by helicopter and be transferred to new posts with insanely high compensation.

---

8. These economic elites make little space for others to be upwardly mobile, and live in fear of the working class becoming conscious, questioning the elites' privileges and looking closely at exactly who is calling the shots behind important political decisions (for example, against a law that guarantees decent work, reduces employment flexibility or increases the minimum wage for young workers).

The old promises of neoliberalism

This feeling of injustice found a powerful outlet in the protests in reaction to the economic and financial crisis. People are disappointed with political responses based on old neoliberal prescriptions: demanding cuts in 'excessive state expenditure', advocating for a tiny, condensed State, cuts in social investments, privatisation of public services, wage, pension and unemployment benefit squeezes and reducing investments in health and education. The revival of the old neoliberal prescriptions pushes countries towards recession and offers little comfort to the 27 million unemployed in the EU, including a significant number of young people. The advocates of austerity say 'let's press forward; we need to swallow bitter pills now to achieve prosperity'. But prosperity for whom? The same policies that caused the crisis are now supposed to contribute towards salvation: tax advantages and incentives to production for large companies for competition's sake, and state guarantees for banks too big to be accountable for their strategic business errors. This policy burden is shouldered by workers, who have to pay the price and 'tighten their belts'.

The Occupy movement went to the streets to denounce the 'dangerous imbalance' created where the population has to pay for the whims of finance capitalism. It gave a voice to the anger and despair of the 99 per cent who are tired of staying below the glass ceiling and paying the debts created by wrong policies. Even with this demonstration of popular discontent, the rating agencies and the mainstream media (like *The Economist*, the *Financial Times*, *Der Spiegel* and *El Mercurio*) continue to advocate neoliberalism as a solution. Even worse, they are on a veritable offensive against states that attempt to follow a different route, refuse the neoliberal recipe and work towards developing a more responsible, cooperative and egalitarian response to the crisis.

Inequality is not a divine curse

The rise of the extreme right in Europe shows us that this attempt to disqualify the responses of the left without offering other solutions is dangerous. This new right is taking advantage of the wave of popular discontent to push their nationalist agendas. But inequality and social imbalance cannot be resolved nationally in today's globalised and interconnected world, and certainly not with the reactionary response of isolation.

There is some good news in the current debate that has been gaining momentum. Inequality is not an inevitable by-product of globalisation or the free movement of labour, capital, goods and services, or of the technological changes that favour better trained and educated salaried workers. Public policies can play a decisive role in defining the direction of development in a society. They can favour a more egalitarian redistribution of wealth, for instance through tax reform promoting progressive taxation and a tax on property. They can promote decent work and equal opportunities regardless of gender, colour, class or sexual orientation. They can make use of instruments to facilitate political and economic participation by a broader section of society. In short, they can define and promote social, economic, environmental and political sustainability.

However, in order to achieve such progressive change, interests and powers will have to be shaken up by a wide-ranging and strong mobilisation of social forces: social movements, the student movement, organised workers, NGOs, feminists, environmentalists, human rights activists, progressive academics and economists, alternative media . . . In short, we must promote dialogue with the many elements of society and deal with this political and ideological struggle for a development project that values wealth distribution and labour, with respect for human rights and a reduction in the gross inequalities that characterise our current social reality. Building these alternatives and coalitions is also an important challenge for the international labour movement.

Trade unions and the building of alternatives

We live in a globalised world, where resistance against the withdrawal of rights is happening in all nations. In the same way that capital and the great powers define their interests beyond all borders, the labour world also needs mechanisms to hold this confrontation, and to exert political pressure on the United Nations (UN), the WTO (World Trade Organisation), the G20 (group of 20 wealthiest countries in the world) or the ILO (International Labour Organisation). The labour movement must leave its niche among organised workers and open itself up to a wider perspective on the problems facing the majority. How do we deal with the challenges of informal work and how do we organise vulnerable workers? How do we position ourselves vis-à-vis transnational companies as a global workers' movement? How do we organise the interests of the whole of the working class and build alliances to advocate for systemic political reforms – such as those related to taxation, taxes on property and guaranteeing rights in an international context? Basically, how do we build a strategic plan for a wider struggle, to design and promote alternatives to neoliberalism and exercise pressure for a change of direction in policy?

Latin America suffered from the misleading ways of neoliberal policies in the 1980s and 1990s – more so than any other continent. It faced hyperinflation, privatisation of state-owned companies and essential services, unemployment and economic instability. However, the hard times made the left and particularly the workers' movement aware that strong alliances among actors of the progressive camp are required in order to fight the majority neoliberal discourse. Only in this way is it possible to build robust, convincing alternatives. This cooperation of the progressive camp prepared some fertile ground for a change in power in our region and has opened a window of opportunities to think about alternatives for dealing with the neoliberal philosophy with a new logic, integrating the economic, social, environmental and political dimensions.

It is no wonder that Brazil's reaction to the 2008/9 crisis was based on a return to public investments and social dialogue. The alliances arising from the struggles of the 1980s and 1990s facilitated this dialogue and opened doors for unions in the context of a more socially sensitive government. The establishment of a national policy to add real value to the minimum wage was a victory for Brazilian unions and for the unity of all the labour congresses, whose pressure led to this policy today being guaranteed by law.

The Development Platform for the Americas (PLADA) of the Trade Union Confederation of the Americas (TUCA) is another good example of the influence of a strategic union policy. Built collectively in consultation with the grassroots, PLADA aims to present a proposal for overcoming the structural imbalances in the region, furthering the transformations achieved in recent years by emancipatory political projects. It will be a platform to organise and mobilise counter-hegemonic forces for the construction of a democracy in which the great majorities will be able to express themselves both via their representatives and through participatory mechanisms.

What is needed at an international level is nothing short of a new progressive consensus that brings together unions, social movements and the left – all those who dare to propel a policy that truly faces up to historical inequalities and creates a society with equal opportunities, where prosperity is shared amongst all and not only a few. With the International Trade Union Confederation (ITUC), the international labour movement can and should be the vehicle for preparing these agendas and convergences. The last congress in Berlin was a good start and showed the united spirit of the working class in fighting neoliberalism and austerity policies. Let's rev up those engines!

Resisting Exploitation and Neoliberalism

16

The Hobbit: An Unexpected Outcome?

Carol Jess

The film industry is an important part of New Zealand culture and a source of patriotic pride, particularly since the successes of Peter Jackson and Weta Workshop with *The Lord of the Rings* films (LOTR). It is also economically significant; in 2004, 150,000 foreign tourists gave *The Lord of the Rings* as one of the main reasons for their visit to New Zealand. Globally, LOTR is the highest grossing motion picture trilogy of all time, and the joint record holder for the number of Oscars. In the run up to the premiere of *The Hobbit – An Unexpected Journey*, a prequel to LOTR, on 28 November 2012, New Zealand went Hobbit mad. Wellington was turned into 'The Middle of Middle Earth' and international visitors received commemorative immigration stamps (Hunt, 2012). For many in the New Zealand trade union movement though, *The Hobbit* has inspired neither pride nor excitement. Instead, the film serves as a reminder of how fragile our rights are when under assault from the fear of capital flight.

The dispute

To understand this (at best) lukewarm reaction, a bit of context is required. The plans to film *The Hobbit* in New Zealand brought to a head an already fairly acrimonious dispute. This involved New Zealand Actors Equity – the union for New Zealand actors – who had been attempting for some time to open negotiations with the Screen Production and Development Association (SPADA), the film industry body. Equity's aim was to update and review a set of minimum terms and conditions for the engagement of actors in screen production in New Zealand concluded in 2005 with SPADA. Frustrated by SPADA's unwillingness to enter into collective bargaining agreements about these, Equity had resorted to industrial action aimed at local television productions. These failed as the producers displayed their willingness to sack the actors and replace them, or even to cancel a whole (final) series of an immensely popular programme (Kelly, 2011). For Equity, the notices for *The Hobbit* production provided an opportunity to break this impasse.

International solidarity

In line with the concept of international solidarity, in June 2010 the International Federation of Actors (FIA) (the actors' Global Union Federation) discussed the New Zealand situation, and made a resolution that their affiliates' members should not 'sign on' to work on *The Hobbit* until collective bargaining was agreed – a step known as 'grey-listing'. Exchanges were made privately between the production company for *The Hobbit* and the unions; word of this 'do not sign' order may never have reached the public, but for what Helen Kelly describes as Peter Jackson's 'nuclear option'. On 27 September 2010, Jackson released a statement in which he condemned the union as an 'Australian bully'[1] looking to wreck the New Zealand film industry to the benefit of its Australian competitors. He also raised the possibility of the film being moved overseas (somewhat vaguely, to Eastern Europe).

There followed a series of very public attacks from Jackson and his production company associates, building on his narrative of unions as an external 'enemy' forcing capital into action. Despite this acrimonious rhetoric, private negotiations between Equity and SPADA continued, and an agreement to bargain was reached on 13 October. This should have been the end of the drama. The stand-off was over, the FIA 'grey-listing' of *The Hobbit* was lifted, and all that remained was to decide on the timing and manner of the public announcement that there was no longer a grey list. But despite a media release being agreed to on 17 October, no announcement was made.

The debacle!

While the union held off on announcing the resolution of the dispute (as inexplicably agreed with SPADA and Warner Bros), Peter Jackson elected

---

1. New Zealand Equity is an independent subsidiary of the Australian Media Arts and Entertainment Association.

to stir the hornets' nest again. Addressing a meeting he had called at Weta Workshops, Jackson announced that the Hobbit dispute was not over, and worse, that Warner Bros executives were coming to New Zealand to prepare to move production overseas. The response from Weta employees was predictable: hostility to the union and fear at the prospect of losing their jobs. Jackson's meeting coincided precisely with a nationwide day of action, organised by the Council of Trade Unions (CTU) to protest against planned changes to employment rights.

Clearly, holding off for a joint statement was no longer an option; Equity issued its own statement explaining that – contrary to Jackson's dire warnings – the 'do not work' order had been rescinded, and that this had been known to everyone involved. This was largely ignored by the New Zealand media, which prominently reported Jackson's version. Faced with a version of events that depicted the unions as driving away *The Hobbit*, many New Zealanders reacted with outrage. Union leaders were subject to an onslaught of abuse, including death threats. Warner Bros executives did indeed come to New Zealand, and were welcomed by the government. The result was confirmation that the filming of *The Hobbit* would take place, after all, in New Zealand. But at a price.

Concessions

The government's concessions were twofold. First, an amendment to the Employment Relations Act 2000 (the overarching legislation regulating employment in New Zealand) was announced on 28 October, and was passed into law the very next day under a process called 'urgency'.[2] This amendment excludes from the statutory definition of 'employee' all those engaged in film production work in any capacity, thus removing any employment rights or protections from any New Zealander engaged in this sector of the economy.

Second, the government made further tax concessions and subsidies to Warner Bros. This may have reflected changes to the exchange rate between the US and New Zealand, which had made New Zealand a less favourable

---

2. Intended for genuine emergencies (such as the Christchurch earthquakes) this allows legislation to be passed through all the Parliamentary stages without any public consultation, Committee stages, or regulatory impact statements.

filming location. It is not impossible, though, that Warner Bros felt their bargaining position strengthened by the tide of pro-Hobbit/anti-union opinion, stirred up by a combination of Jackson's threats and the media's portrayal of events.

Conclusion

The on-going release of documents under New Zealand's freedom of information legislation throws light on just how well manipulated the union, the media and the public were over this dispute. But the ease with which the internationally-recognised rights of workers to collectively bargain and organise were swept away overnight is symptomatic of a climate in which the narrative of trade unions, and their members, as the 'other', 'foreign' and a threat to 'our' economy, jobs and livelihoods has taken root. This narrative is particularly powerful when taken up by such a Kiwi 'icon' as Peter Jackson. Jackson was not a disinterested, neutral party in this case – but his motives and actions were never scrutinised or questioned. He, a multi-millionaire, Hollywood 'player', was depicted as 'one of us', union members as the 'other'.

Since 2010, further industrial disputes throughout New Zealand have been met with the same treatment, ensuring that already bitter arguments over the place (and pace) of casualisation, 'flexibility' and job insecurity are framed to ensure anyone arguing for maintenance of employment rights and protections is seen as a threatening 'other' (Maritime Union of New Zealand, 2012; Grocott, 2012). Possibly emboldened by the ease with which they were able to rewrite employment law for film workers, the New Zealand government now plans further anti-union legislation. Its new proposals include removing the requirement for an agreement to be reached in collective bargaining. Without this requirement, the disputes noted above would not have occurred, as the management could simply have walked away from bargaining, sacking and replacing the union workers.[3]

Meanwhile, living standards for the majority in New Zealand continue to fall, as the cost of living continues to rise and inequality widens (Service and Food Workers Union, 2012). The threat to the 'ordinary Kiwi' does not lie

---

3. The Employment Relations Amendment Act 2014 was one of the first bills to be passed after the return to Government of the National party at the general election on 20 September 2014.

in the retention of what few employment rights they have, but the actions of those who profit from the on-going march of neoliberalism, and the culture of fear and insecurity they rely on.

References

Dominion Post. (2010) 'The show will go on – wherever it is', *Stuff*. Available from www.stuff.co.nz.

Grocott, M. (2012) 'MPs rally to meatworkers' cause', *Stuff*. Available from www.stuff.co.nz.

Haworth, N. (2012) 'A Political Economy of *The Hobbit*', *Dispute Journal of Employment Relations*, Vol. 36, No. 3.

Hunt, T. (2012). 'Middle-earth-returns-for-The-Hobbit', *Stuff*. Available from www.stuff.co.nz.

Kelly, K. (2011) 'The Hobbit Dispute', *Scoop*. Available from http://scoop.co.nz.

Maritime Union of New Zealand (2012) 'Ports of Auckland dispute about job security – not wages', *Maritime Union of New Zealand*. Available from www.munz.org.nz.

McAndrew, I. and Risak, M.E. (2012) 'Shakedown in the Shaky Isles: Union bashing', *New Zealand Labor Studies Journal*, Vol. 37, No. 1.

Mosley, L. and Uno, S. (2007) 'Racing to the Bottom or Climbing to the Top? Economic Globalisation and Collective Labor Rights Comparative', *Political Studies* Vol. 40, No. 8.

Nutall, P. (2012) 'Where the Shadows lie: Confusions, misunderstanding and misinformation about workplace status', *New Zealand Journal of Employment Relations*, Vol. 36, No. 3.

PriceWaterhouseCoopers (2009) 'Economic contribution of the New Zealand film and television industry', *PriceWaterhouseCoopers*. Available from www.jimca.co.jp.

Service and Food Workers Union (2012) 'Stats show shocking truth of growing inequality in NZ', *Scoop*. Available from www.scoop.co.nz.

Tyson, A.F. (2012) 'A Synopsis of the Hobbit Dispute', *New Zealand Journal of Employment Relations*, Vol. 36, No. 3.

Wilkinson, K. (2012) 'One Law to Rule them All', *New Zealand Journal of Employment Relations*, Vol. 36, No. 3.

17

Right to Work and Michigan Labour

Roland Zullo

The incorporated right to work (RTW) movement has scored a major victory in Michigan. On the heels of the 2012 election, during a lame duck session in which house Republicans held a 64 to 46 advantage over Democrats, the Michigan legislature passed two bills; one to enact RTW for public sector unions and the other for private sector unions. The private sector bill passed 58 to 52, with no votes from Democrats, and was quickly signed into law by Governor Rick Snyder without any formal public discussion or debate. Nefariously, the law was attached to an appropriations bill, which by Michigan law prevents opponents from taking the issue to a popular referendum.[4] Thus, RTW became central to the partisan dialogue leading up to the 2014 election. Organised labour mobilised to 'reward friends and punish enemies' at the ballot box in an effort to unseat incumbents that passed RTW law, with Governor Snyder the highest profiled target. However, Labour's efforts fell short and Snyder won re-election, capturing 51 per cent of the vote against Democratic challenger Mark Schauer, who garnered 47 per cent of the vote. And Republicans picked up two seats in the Michigan Senate and four seats in the Michigan House of Representatives, further solidifying control over these legislative chambers. The 2014 election outcome has implications for Michigan and the US mid-west region.

Right to work: representation without taxation

First, to appreciate why RTW is controversial – why labour opposes RTW and corporate activists spend lavishly to pass RTW – one must understand the legal distinction between 'bargaining unit member' and 'union member'

---

4. Republican supporters of RTW had reasons for employing this tactic. In 2012, a popular referendum was used to overturn the Emergency Manager Law, also supported by
   Republicans and signed by Snyder. Polling in Michigan generally shows that when the
   issue is explained, the majority of citizens oppose RTW laws.

in US labour law. The two classifications are not equivalent and persons in the bargaining unit are not compelled to be union members. In the US, to simplify labour-management relations and limit union raiding, labour unions have the exclusive right to negotiate on behalf of the bargaining unit members they organise. Unions do not, however, determine bargaining unit composition. The National Labor Relations Board (NLRB), or similar agency at the state level holds final judgement over bargaining unit membership, where determination is based on 'community of interest' criteria; for example similar skills, proximity, management oversight, and so forth. At any given workplace, if a job matches those criteria, the person holding that job becomes part of the bargaining unit, regardless of how that individual may feel about unionisation. Then, if a majority of workers in the prospective bargaining unit unionise (usually through a government supervised election), the new organisation must represent all fairly and without prejudice. This '50 per cent plus 1' method of determining union coverage nearly guarantees the presence of a minority group opposing unionisation. Further, often a person gains union coverage by accepting employment at a worksite that is already unionised, without ever having the opportunity to vote for or against unionisation, and these individuals might also oppose unionisation.

Once a bargaining unit is organised, unions cannot deny representation services to persons in the unit who do not want to be union members; discriminatory behaviour is discouraged by civil lawsuits under duty of fair representation provisions. Thus a union is obligated, for instance, to defend a non-member during a disciplinary hearing which, if the case goes to arbitration, might cost the union tens of thousands of dollars. Bargaining unit members who refrain from becoming union members lose some rights, for example they cannot vote in union leadership elections or run for union office, but they obtain all the benefits and protections in the labour-management contract.

So what happens to a bargaining unit member who rejects union membership? In a non-RTW state, a labour union and employer can negotiate a range of contract provisions (called union security clauses) that require covered persons to pay dues. Unions want union security clauses because they are an efficient method for collecting the finances necessary to run their organisations. In non-RTW states, unions typically prefer 'union shop' terms that require every person benefiting from representation to pay union dues. At a minimum, represented non-members are required to pay an amount that covers the expense of negotiating and administering the labour agreement (referred to as collective bargaining activities). In RTW states, the parties are barred from negotiating union security clauses, making the default the 'open shop', where the payment of dues by bargaining unit members is optional. Between these two policy poles are arrangements that require covered persons to pay a proportion of full dues, or even to allow objectors to contribute dues to charity. Such arrangements are, however, proscribed under the new Michigan law.

This extended explanation is needed to clarify what the phrase 'right to work' means. In the US, RTW has little to do with the right of a person to seek and accept gainful employment. The phrase has dubious origins, but scholars have linked the term with the corporate 'open shop' movement of the early twentieth century, which aimed to weaken unions by encouraging 'at-will' employment terms; contracts, usually unwritten, between individuals and employers. Corporate US has historically advocated for the 'freedom' of individual contract when faced with the threat of collective action by workers. Prohibiting union security clauses and thus allowing persons to refrain from financially supporting labour unions does favour the individual over the collective. As with any tax, the collection of dues is coercive from the perspective of the objector. Yet once union security clauses are in place, non-payment of dues can become a dischargeable offence. Someone seeking to avoid paying union dues in that context has three options: (1) exit their job, (2) convince union leadership to negotiate an open shop, or (3) persuade fellow workers to decertify the union. The viable option for dissenters is to work elsewhere. Thus the full definition of RTW is the right to reap the benefits of collective representation at work without having to contribute toward the cost of obtaining those benefits. Labour unions prefer the phrase 'right to freeload'.

Killing institutionalised collective worker power

Conceptually what is at work is Mancur Olson's (1965) economic-based theory on collective action. Any organisation producing a non-excludable good must contend with the classic collective action problem: how to finance organisational activities when persons with access to the good have an incentive to refrain from paying.[5] The existence of 'free riders' – persons who enjoy the good without contributing – reduces resources, causing the organisation to underperform in its objectives. And by increasing the cost burden for persons who contribute, free-riders decrease the likelihood of organisational formation, and hasten organisational extinction. Union representation in the workplace is a non-excludable good, since all persons in a bargaining unit, members and objectors are entitled to the rights and benefits of coverage. For organised labour, RTW laws exacerbate the collective action problem by making it easy for persons benefitting from union representation to refrain from paying toward its cost. Consistent with Olson's theory, unions are weaker and less effective in RTW states.

In application, unions are affected in two general ways by RTW law. First, because objectors pay nothing, unions suffer a direct reduction in dues revenue. The average loss is around 15 per cent, but this figure can vary widely across contexts. In cases where unionists have a strong craft identity, RTW will have a minimal effect on membership rates. In situations where there is rapid employment turnover (e.g. grocery industry) or significant internal membership conflict, the figure will be greater. Unions that have especially high turnover, such as graduate student unions, might simply fold. It remains to be seen how RTW will affect the United Auto Workers (UAW) in Michigan, given the 2008 agreement that resulted in a two-tier wage system, whereby new hires receive hourly pay that is roughly half of senior members. Two-tier wages were a condition placed on the 2008 auto bailout, and a difficult pill to swallow for the UAW. Disparity in compensation between first- and second-tier members may now motivate defection among workers in the second tier; it will certainly pressure the UAW to close the wage rate gap.

Second, RTW changes the way that unions spend resources. Unions in RTW states must continually organise represented persons in order to sustain an active membership and recruit objectors. One might argue such activities make the union more responsive to members (a line frequently invoked by advocates of RTW), but there is no convincing evidence that covered persons are better off in RTW states. Unions in RTW states often hold more social gatherings or might take on projects meant to impress

---

5. 'Non-excludable good' refers to products or services that, once developed, can be broadly accessed or enjoyed by persons who had no role in creating or financing the good.

members, rather than advance the labour movement. One of the most commonly voiced objections to unions made by bargaining unit members is that resources are spent to elect undesirable politicians or to advance unworthy causes. The RTW laws enable disgruntled bargaining unit members to withhold their dues based on such objections. The organisation becomes member-focused, as opposed to movement-focused, and activities such as political advocacy and new member organising decline. Indeed, reducing organised labour's political power in society is the main agenda behind the RTW movement.

Declining labour standards for the US mid-west

The 2014 election results seal RTW into Michigan's foreseeable future. Moreover, Republican dominance in the Michigan legislature could mean a further erosion of bargaining rights for public employees. In 2011, the Republican controlled legislature prohibited bargaining over numerous subjects of interest to public school unions, such as the outsourcing of school support functions, teacher evaluation, and teacher placement.[6] Similar restrictions could be extended to other public employee classifications in the municipal sectors or state agencies. An extreme measure would be the full repeal of public sector bargaining rights.

The 2014 election has implications beyond Michigan. For the mid-west region, the Michigan results signalled that it is possible to enact anti-labour reform in a heavily unionised state and succeed at the ballot box. An emboldened RTW movement will likely target Wisconsin, another historically unionised state, where Republicans currently control the legislature and citizens re-elected a Tea Party-endorsed Republican governor. Republican Bruce Rauner, the newly elected governor of Illinois proposed 'employee empowerment zones' in his 4 February 2015 State of the State speech, whereby '[t]hese zones will give employees the freedom to choose whether or not they want to join a union'. As each state lowers labour standards by adopting RTW, surrounding states are pressured to follow. Achieving RTW across the industrial mid-west, where much of the US labour movement originated, would be a stunning achievement for the incorporated RTW movement.

---

6. See Michigan Public Act 25 of 2011.

References

Olson, M. (1965) *The Logic of Collective Action: Public Goods and the Theory of Groups* (Cambridge, MA: Harvard University Press).

18

A Site of Struggle: Organised Labour and Domestic Worker Organising in Mozambique

Ruth Castel-Branco

Although rooted in colonialism, domestic work has become a hallmark of modern urban living in Mozambique. There are more than 39,000 registered domestic workers living in and around Maputo – a 30 per cent increase in ten years – and domestic work has become the most important occupation for urban women, after self-employment (INE, 2007). So vital is domestic work to Maputo's economy that when the Mozambican state moved to extend labour protection to domestic workers in 2008, the Ministry of Labour removed minimum wage language for fear that employers, many of whom are themselves minimum wage earners, would no longer be able to participate in the labour force.

Despite the importance of paid domestic work, organised labour has historically paid little attention to this sector. In contrast to South Africa, where the extension of labour protections to domestic workers was seen as key to redressing the injustices of apartheid and engendering democracy, in Mozambique this was outside Frelimo's – and thus the *Organização dos Trabalhadores Moçambicanos*'s (Mozambican Workers' Organisation – OTM) – political imagination.

This chapter explores why domestic work is a strategic growth area for organised labour in Mozambique, arguing that ultimately, unions are themselves sites of struggle between competing interests and visions, capable of shifting direction, strategies and tactics.

Organised labour reorients

Three workers' organisations currently represent domestic workers in Maputo: the *Sindicato de EmpregadosDomésticos de Moçambique* (Mozambican Domestic Workers' Association – SEDOMO), the *Associação das Mulheres Empregadas Domésticas* (Women's Association of Domestic Workers – AMUEDO), and the *Sindicato Nacional de Empregados Domésticos* (National Union of Domestic Workers – SINED). All are affiliated with one of two labour federations.

Asked why organised labour has shifted attention towards the informal economy in general, and domestic work in particular, the coordinator of OTM's Women's Workers Committee responds:

> In Mozambique the unions have had a strong interest in the informal sector for a while. When the factories closed many former OTM members had no recourse but to turn to the informal sector. OTM recognised this and pushed for the formalisation of these sectors. (Interview with COMUTRA coordinator, 23 June 2011)

However, the secretary general of AMUEDO contends that OTM was reluctant to organise domestic workers because of the dispersed and private nature of the workplace. Isolated behind closed doors, domestic workers are invisible to the outside world, inaccessible to labour inspectors or organisers, and outnumbered in the household. This makes them prone to abuse and difficult to organise. Live-in workers are particularly vulnerable as they rely on their employers for a place to live. 'When we had regional seminars, the issue always came up. "It would have been easier if it were three or four companies," they said. "But imagine organising domestic workers flat-by-flat in all these buildings in Maputo"' (interview with AMUEDO general secretary, 1 July 2011).

By 2007 OTM had joined forces with AMUEDO and lawyers at the Ministry of Labour to draft *Decree 40/2008*, extending labour protections to domestic workers for the first time since independence. Domestic workers now have the right to a written contract, set schedule, daily break, weekly and annual leave, and social protection. Why did OTM change its mind?

Reasons for reorientation

The shift began almost two decades earlier. Hit hard by Mozambique's economic restructuring at the end of the 1980s, OTM's membership dropped from 300,000 to 90,000 between the 1980s and 2003. The 1990 constitutional reforms that democratised the labour movement and delinked OTM from the state further weakened the federation. As the federation faced rising pressure from its membership to take action against the exploitative practices of newly privatised companies, it found itself without the capacity to respond. This compromised OTM's position among its membership, sowing the seeds for a divided labour movement. In 1992, three unions split to form the independent federation known today as the *Confederação Nacional dos Sindicatos Independentes e Livres de Moçambique* (CONSILMO). It was in this context that the informal economy became a strategic growth area for OTM.

However, the real push came when leaders from its own ranks began independently to organise domestic workers into an association. Maputo's first association of domestic workers was AMUEDO, formalised in 2006 by a former OTM leader. When OTM discovered she was recruiting domestic workers to the association, she was suspended. Once expelled, she affiliated AMUEDO with the rival federation CONSILMO. In response, OTM founded its own domestic workers' association, SEDOMO.

While AMUEDO maintains that the creation of SEDOMO was an attempt by OTM to undermine their work, SEDOMO argues that this was a natural process for OTM. 'OTM was already fielding calls for help from domestic workers. The inclusion of domestic workers in the labour law was OTM's idea' (interview with COMUTRA coordinator, 23 June 2011).

Shortly after, a third worker organisation, SINED, was formed and affiliated with OTM. SINED began informally in 2006 and was formalised in 2008.

In 2008 the International Labour Organisation placed 'Decent Work for Domestic Workers' on the International Labour Conference agenda for 2010 and 2011. The campaign to adopt and now ratify Convention 189 galvanised domestic workers organising in Maputo, a focus for mobilisation, and with access to external resources through ITUC, IDWN and SINED. As one OTM official disclosed: 'Each donor has its own philosophy, its own programme that it will fund, so we generally try to be flexible, to gear our programme to what is being funded' (interview with SINED secretary for international relations, 30 July 2011).

Shifting strategies and tactics

Workers' organisations have played a critical role in advancing domestic workers' rights. They have increased the visibility of this sector and sought to change how employers perceive domestic workers. Organising models have also shifted in response to the peculiarities of domestic work. Taxi ranks, parks and street corners have been transformed into centres of recruitment, mobilisation and political education. Domestic workers are trained to engage in dialogue with their employers. Workers' organisations emphasise dialogue and conciliation, as a strategy to preserve the employment relationship in a context of asymmetrical power relations: 'No one wins if a domestic worker is dismissed. If it comes to mediation, we speak in a soft tone; we try to understand employers' point of view; we try to remind both parties of the long history they've had together' (interview with SINED secretary for international relations, 30 July 2011).

One domestic worker explains her strategy:

> Pick a day when you see that your employer is calm and explain your problem . . . if he tries to justify his actions, to elevate himself, you need to bow down to him because he can't accept that you're equals. You'll have your time to talk to him, but you shouldn't get into a heated discussion. (Interview with Josina, 16 June 2012)

Though conditions are negotiated one-on-one between worker and employer, guided by common goals, they take on a collective character.

Looking forward

It is too early to predict the impact of this new wave of organising. Despite optimism, domestic worker organising has become a battleground for autonomy, power and resources, with potentially detrimental effects. Despite almost identical demands, strategies and tactics, AEDOMO, AMUEDO and SINED do not communicate, let alone collaborate. Deeply entrenched competition and distrust between workers' organisations has further fuelled domestic workers' scepticism of unions, making recruitment challenging. Asked why she refuses to collaborate with the other organisation, AMUEDO secretary general responds: 'I started first. SINED and AEDOMO don't know anything. OTM has set them up to demoralise and weaken AMUEDO' (interview with AMUEDO General Secretary, 1 July 2011).

Unions are also challenged by lack of funding, and often lose organisers when they are recruited to other sectors. Union statistics put unionised domestic workers at 10,000. Despite constraint, domestic workers' associations have the potential to profoundly affect working conditions in this sector.

References

Boletim da República (2008) *Decreto No. 40/2008: Regulamento do Trabalho Doméstico*, I Serie, Numero 48, Maputo, República de Moçambique.

INE (2007) 'III General Population Census' *Instituto Nacional de Estatística*, Maputo, Mozambique. Interview with AMUEDO General Secretary (1 July 2011), R. Castel-Branco, Maputo, Mozambique.

Interview with COMUTRA Coordinator (23 June 2012), R. Castel-Branco, Maputo, Mozambique.

Interview with Josina (16 June 2012), R. Castel-Branco, Maputo, Mozambique.

Interview with SINED Secretary for International Relations (30 July 2011)., R. Castel-Branco, Maputo, Mozambique.

19

Constructing an anti-Neoliberal Analysis to Arrive at Truly Alternative Alternatives

Salimah Valiani

For the past few decades the world economy has been shifting through radical restructuring and reorganisation. Within this context, the 'anti-globalisation', 'anti-WTO', 'anti-neoliberal', and other such movements are an important field within which to identify the thinking behind the action. For Antonio Gramsci (1971), questions of theory and practice are raised particularly when the 'movement of historical transformation is at its most rapid'. The point of such questioning, as Gramsci says, is to make the 'practical forces unleashed' more efficient and expansive and the 'theoretical programmes' more realistically justified. Taking inspiration from this, the aim of this chapter is to provide methodological direction in analysing and responding to changes in the neoliberal era using the instance of the global restructuring of nursing labour markets.

Analysing neoliberal globalisation

Unlike mainstream economists, Marxists and post-Marxists have long viewed capitalism as a global process. The starting point of this process has been a topic of debate, with some arguing it began as far back as the sixteenth century and others arguing it began in the nineteenth century. Within these historical approaches the changes of the past few decades can be linked to underlying contradictions and cycles in the world capitalist economy.

In *The Long Twentieth Century*, Giovanni Arrighi (1994) traces four 'systemic cycles of accumulation' in the history of the capitalist world economy. These are: the Genoese cycle (circa 1450–1640), the Dutch cycle (circa 1640–1790), the British cycle (circa 1790–1925) and the US cycle (circa 1925–present). Within each cycle of accumulation, a phase of 'material expansion' is followed by a phase of 'financial expansion'. A phase of material expansion consists of continuous change whereby the capitalist world economy grows steadily along a well-defined path under the leadership of a hegemonic state. A phase of financial expansion consists of discontinuous change whereby the established path has reached its limits, the hegemonic state loses power over capitalists and other interest groups, and the world economy shifts onto a new path via radical restructuring and reorganisation.

The financial expansion of Arrighi's 'US cycle of accumulation' begins circa 1970. In concrete terms, the clampdown on workers' rights and diminished recognition of unions around the world, moves by large pharmaceutical corporations to patent Southern seeds and medicinal plants, the formation of the World Trade Organisation – can all be seen as instances of restructuring and reorganisation resulting from limits of the material expansion of circa 1950–70.

In terms of Gramsci's 'practice' or 'action', rather than simply denouncing the neoliberal trend of the past few decades, we should seek to uncover the limits and contradictions arising in what is commonly referred to as the 'Golden Age' of capitalism (circa 1950–70). These limits and contradictions are at the heart of the shift to anti-labour, pro-employer policies by the early 1980s. Recognising and examining these contradictions in their specific forms, for example, industry by industry, allows us to search for alternative structures of social organisation and production which have the potential of undoing inequality within and between countries – historic features of the world economy which were far from dismantled during the so-called Golden Age.

Unions and NGOs, especially in the global North, tend to rely on ahistorical, economistic analytic tools. The key shortcomings of these tools are the assumptions that national labour and other markets are separate rather than globally interconnected, and that active states can steer the behaviour of firms in favour of the good of the public regardless of the extent of corporate power. A rarely defined 'globalisation' is thus identified as cause and/or effect of a wide range of phenomena: from 'free trade' agreements, to the over-exploitation of natural resources, to austerity measures, to precarisation of work. The solutions proposed amount to a return to the Keynesian model of the Golden Age – despite the fact that the current world political-economic context is vastly different and such a return is highly unlikely.

The global shift to temporary nurse migration and its roots in capitalist contradictions

Using Arrighi's framework of cycles of accumulation, along with conceptual tools of Marxian economics, the shift from permanent to temporary nurse migration may be understood as the outcome of contradictions which arose during the so-called Golden Age of capitalism. In the 1990s, employers in the global North began favouring the employment of internationally educated nurses on temporary work permits. This was a shift from internationally educated nurses entering the North on a permanent basis, with the rights to settle and sponsor family members, choose one's place of residence and employment, and legal protection under all laws pertaining to locally based workers. In most countries of the North, permanent migration of internationally educated nurses – and indeed, internationally educated workers of most occupations – was the norm from 1950 to 1990. In the health care industry, both then and now, the majority of migrant workers originate in the global South, hence the importance of permanent migration whereby migrating workers can benefit from relatively better working conditions and social possibilities in the North.

As I argue in *Rethinking Unequal Exchange: The Global Integration of Nursing Labour Markets* (2012), Canada and the United States were the first countries of the global North to begin employing large numbers of internationally educated nurses on temporary work permits. The reasons for this shift are rooted in different capitalist contradictions. In the US it is ultimately due to the monopoly structure of medical technology production that hospital employers turned to cost saving strategies in the area of nursing labour in the late 1980s. Various cost-cutting measures had been attempted to counter hospital cost escalation from the 1970s, but with little success. Though medical technology was identified as a cost pusher by the early 1990s, due to the political inability of a capitalist state to challenge the small group of capitalists dominating the medical technology industry from the 1950s, hospitals opted to reduce costs by replacing registered nurses (i.e. four-year university trained) with lesser trained health workers, and by employing lesser paid temporary migrant registered nurses. Being largely female, the nursing labour force was politically far less powerful than medical technology producers or even physicians, though nurse unionisation had increased steadily in the US in the 1980s.

Two major contradictions of the Golden Age can be drawn from the US instance: (1), the monopolistic tendency in the material expansion of the US cycle of accumulation in which small groups of companies came to dominate industries through varying combinations of horizontal and vertical integration, and (2), the dependency of states and populations on goods produced by these private interests, including in the area of health care, an area of major state investment during the Golden Age as part of Keynesian welfare state development.

In Canada, though nurses are the only health professionals serving patients 24 hours a day, seven days a week, in all areas of health care, this predominantly female labour force has been historically undervalued. Since inception in the late 1960s, Canada's public health care system has contained expenditures through the undervaluing and overworking of nurses. The increased use of temporary migrant nursing labour is one of several developments arising from this contradiction. In brief, when overextended, Canada-based nurses both stopped working as nurses, and began migrating in unprecedented numbers. From the late 1980s, Canada began employing relatively large numbers of temporary migrant nurses. In the early 2000s, the employment of lesser-paid, temporary migrant nurses began rising again as political pressures to contain public health care costs became more pronounced.

This analysis paves the way for action and advocacy which go beyond calling for ratification/enforcement of International Labour Organisation (ILO) conventions and other legal instruments protecting migrant workers' rights, or calling for regulation of nurse recruitment agencies – the major responses by health worker unions to date. In the US, this analysis points to a possible strategy of campaigning for the socialised production of medical technology to cut continually escalating health care costs and redirect funds towards bedside nursing care. Socialised production of pharmaceuticals could be similarly proposed by health worker unions as a solution to cost and other excesses of the pharmaceutical industry – the other major cause of unsustainable cost escalation in health systems not only in the US but around the world (Valiani, 2012).

In Canada, the analysis here points to the urgent need – if we systematically believe in equality – to confront the nexus of capitalism and patriarchy which makes for the consistent undervaluing of nursing and other caring labour around the world. The fundamental contradiction of the Golden Age at play here is that public-financed health care systems internationally were dependent on undervalued caring labour while aiming to increase wellbeing for all. In essence it is this undervaluing which drives nurses to migrate in search of better wages and working conditions.

Engaging the conditions of restructuring through this type of sector-specific approach is an alternative to super-imposing reformist solutions to deeply entrenched inequalities. World historical and Marxian analysis, on a sector-by-sector basis could provide for creative strategies which

move beyond calls for the return to legal and political structures of a past
long gone.

References

Arrighi, G. (1994) *The Long Twentieth Century* (London: Verso).
Gramsci, A. (1971) *Selections from the Prison Notebooks*, edited and translated
by Q. Hoare and G. Nowell Smith (New York: International Publishers).
Valiani, S. (2012) *Rethinking Unequal Exchange: The Global Integration of
Nursing Labour Markets* (Toronto: University of Toronto Press).

20

The 2012 Strike Wave, Marikana and the History of Rock Drillers in South African Mines

Paul Stewart

After gold was discovered in South Africa in 1886, rock drillers rapidly
established themselves as an elite occupational group. A century ago, rock
drillers on the North American Lake Superior copper mines similarly
enjoyed 'superior status'. They were 'the working class elite' and went on
strike when their status was challenged (Lankton, 1991). This occupational
tradition continues into the present.

Rock drillers have consequently long manifested a specific occupational
culture resulting directly from their central productive role underground.
Due to this role and their objectively-located social power, rock drillers
historically received differential treatment in mining globally. This is the
basis for the platinum rock-drill operator-led strikes since February 2012
and at Marikana in August 2012 where 34 mineworkers were shot dead
by police, precipitating a social crisis and triggering the long-threatened

down-grading of South Africa's financial trading rating on the international market (Khoza, 2012).

Hand drilling and the Jack-Hammer Hands

Drilling is the most central work activity in the support, drill and blast cycle in mining and embodies considerable tacit, experiential and practical skill. Respected within mining communities, rock drillers perform the hardest job and face the most hazardous conditions underground (Alexander et al., 2012). Yet despite being on the lower levels of the job-grading system defining wages and salaries, rock drillers often earned more than supervisors. No other occupation, for instance, earns a special allowance of R750 (€75) for simply doing their job.

The rock drillers were originally described as Jack-Hammer Hands or later simply as 'hammer boys'. These men drilled the rock by hand. Since the introduction of the machine rock drill, they are known as 'machine operators' or RDOs.

The occupation has a distinct origin. The first rock drillers were largely former globally-mobile Cornish tin miners. Only these skilled craftsmen could drill the Witwatersrand Basin's hard quartzite host rock. They worked a month-long contract and uniquely contracted themselves via a verbal agreement with the mine manager based on specific production targets and commanded high wages.

The jack hammerers worked in pairs and drilled with a hammer and chisels. With every hammer blow, the 'Jack' would twist the chisel before the 'Hammer' would deliver the next powerful blow. To drill a hole of 36-inches-a-shift was the norm then for a fair day's work. Engineering designs of the rotary drill were to emulate the twisting motion of the human hand in the design of the 'jack-hammer' machine drill bearing the name of these early hand rock drillers, a job which had already been taken over by black mineworkers by 1897.

Indentured Chinese rock drillers

The black hammer-boys' ranks swelled between 1903 and 1907 when Chinese labourers, of whom between 65 and 70 per cent were rock drillers, were indentured onto the South African gold fields. Being industrious, engineers used them to increase the area mined and decrease the stope-width at rock faces where the support, drill and blast production cycle takes place. This enabled the output of cleaner ore and improved the grade of the low-grade ore-body. The impact of Chinese labour during a severe profitability crisis was consequently '*dramatic, rapid and successful*' (Richardson, 1982).

That Chinese workers enabled narrower stope-widths is significant. Stope-widths today are considerably narrower than they were a century ago. The dimensions of a modern back-fill stope, over three kilometres underground, reveal the cramped nature of this working environment. The stope-width is from 80cm. The depth of the stope is approximately 170cm. The length of the stope is generally between 30 to 40 metres and runs at an angle of between 15 and 30 degrees and has a target ambient temperature of 28.5 degrees Celsius. Drilling horizontally into the rock face here is taxing, rigorous and dangerous, hence its status and the social attitudes it engenders.

The Mozambican workers who replaced the Chinese labourers were to constitute the backbone of the industry for the next 70 years and dominated the rock drillers' occupation, drilling by hand or hand-held machine. A century ago Mozambican hand rock drillers expressed their objective power rooted in production by refusing to drill more than one hole per day as this could become the norm for a day's work.

The hand-held machine rock drill

In 1907, the stand-up 'Slogger' machine rock drill was replaced by the considerably more effective hand-held machine rock drill, even though hand drilling remained the dominant method of breaking rock through to the 1930s. Crucially, neither the hand-held machine drill, nor the process of stoping, has changed appreciably ever since. The hand-held machine rock drill continues to occupy centre stage underground as the working faces, in both gold and platinum mines, have remained stubbornly resistant to mechanisation. With full mechanisation effectively stalled in gold mines and not generalised on platinum mines, the consequence is the continued presence and need of large numbers of workers underground, with the RDOs in particular here to stay for the foreseeable future.

The 'kings of the mine': on strike and in control of production

The status of rock drillers is not only related to the difficulties and critical position of their work, but also because they earned relatively high wages. Rock drillers were never part of the highly contested 'maximum average system' which placed a ceiling, from 1913 to 1965, on black mineworkers' wages (Moodie, 2005). In the 1930s, for instance, the RDOs were viewed by their peers as the 'kings of the mine' due to both the rigour of their work and their earnings which were higher than their immediate supervisors.

The epithet of being 'kings of the mine' surfaced again in 1985. Dissatisfied with their job grade, wage levels and the National Union of Mineworkers (NUM), a group of RDOs confirmed their social power by compelling management on an Anglo Platinum shaft to meet a delegation from their ranks who improved their working conditions. By 1999 the RDOs had formed their own informal workers' committees and over 3,600 of them struck across Anglo Platinum. They were accompanied by a new small trade union representing them, reminiscent of what occurred in 2012 on the platinum mines. This smaller union, around which controversy reigned, the Mouth Peace Workers Union, only managed to gain a foothold among their ranks as they had not been adequately serviced by NUM. Trade union rivalry and violence spilled across the gold and platinum mines.

When 400 RDOs on an Anglo Platinum shaft went on a series of 'RDO strikes' in 2004, they were dismissed. In these strikes the RDOs used violent tactics against other workers and lost supervisors their anticipated Christmas bonus. Tensions were acute on the shaft as the RDOs clung to their unrecognised informal committees as again recently occurred. In 2012, however, the RDOs did not alienate fellow workers, but brought them out on strike instead. Whether these workers collectively understand themselves as a 'vanguard' is not known, although one RDO asserts that 'if RDOs were to decide not to work for a day, the whole mine will be on a standstill'.

In 2004 at the Anglo Platinum shaft, however, after much discussion between all parties and an external facilitator, a productivity deal was negotiated in which the RDOs were the central players. The situation was 'normalised'. Productivity increased by 14 per cent on the shaft, sustained over eight months. Through their own intensified efforts, the RDOs won back their wages and the company won back lost production. No other occupational group could have done this.

Recent strikes on the platinum mines

Following a series of occupations and sit-ins since 2009, in February 2012, at Impala Platinum, 5,000 rock drill operators led twelve other mineworkers out on strike after they were overlooked for a wage increase. With their historically entrenched status ignored by both management and NUM, these RDOs took action and triggered what became the most extensive strike wave in South African mining history (Hattingh, 2010). In August at Lonmin's Marikana mines, 3,000 RDOs followed the Impala RDOs' example, but not before management at Lonmin's Karee mine followed long established practice – negotiating with a delegation of rock drill operators outside of established bargaining structures and granted pay increases (Sosibo, 2012). Taking umbrage that their historically entrenched status was ignored, RDOs at the two other Lonmin mines took action and triggered what became the most extensive strike wave in South African mining history. Other mineworkers across the platinum and gold mines, as well as sporadically on the collieries and elsewhere, including on farms, arguably took the RDOs actions as their cue to wage a series of often violent legally-unprotected wage strikes and articulate other demands. If what is becoming known as the post-Marikana period in South African history is to be understood, the central role of the RDOs in production and the status their job has generated over a century is where any analysis must start.

References

Alexander, P., Lekgowa, T., Mmpoe, B., Dinwell L. and Xezwi B. (2012) *Marikana: A view From the Mountain and a Case to Answer* (Johannesburg: Jacana).

Hattingh, S. (2010) 'Mineworkers Direct Action: Occupations and sit-ins in South Africa', *Working USA: The Journal of Labor and Society*, Vol. 13, September.

Khoza, R. (2012) 'SA bonds close to "junk" level', *Sunday Times, Business Times*, 9 December.

Lankton, L. (1991) *Cradle to Grave: Life, Work, and Death at the Lake Superior Copper Mines* (New York and Oxford: Oxford University Press).

Moodie, D.T. (2005) 'Maximum average Violence: Underground Assaults on the South African gold mines, 1913–1965', *Journal of Southern African Studies*, Vol. 31, No 3.

Richardson, P. (1982) *Chinese Mine Labour in the Transvaal* (London: Macmillan).

Sosibo, K. (2012) 'Lonmin cut deal with rock drillers', *Mail and Guardian*, December 7–13.

Good Samaritans?
Institutional Responses
to Labour Right Abuses

21

Where is Decent Work in DfID Policy? Marketisation and Securitisation of UK International Aid

Phoebe V. Moore

Nothing is spared. Even international development policy is marketised and securitised in the United Kingdom. Outreach to areas of the world suffering from tsunami-related devastation has not disappeared, but recent government decisions reveal significant shifts for aid spending to prioritise future conflict prevention in areas facing high levels of unemployment and lacking welfare protection, and to manage future financial impacts of terrorist attacks. Controversially, UK aid spending is increasing in areas where crisis-driven unemployment can be linked to rising social unrest, even as cuts are made to the organisation most dedicated to advocating workers' rights, the International Labour Organisation (ILO).

DfID securitises, marketises international aid

In March 2011 the Department for International Development (DfID) published the 'Multilateral Aid Review: Ensuring Maximum Value for Money for UK Aid Through Multilateral Organisations' (DfID, 2011). In 2010 the UK's newly-elected coalition government decided to increase development aid to 0.7 per cent of gross national income (GNI) by 2013, which is, in cash terms, an increase from £7.8 billion in 2010–11 to £11 billion in 2014–15. In that context, DfID, in cooperation with then Secretary of State for International Development, Andrew Mitchell, reviewed 43 multilateral aid organisations previously used to channel aid funding using a specific methodology designed to measure organisations' aims and objectives, *value for money* and *cost effectiveness*. UN-HABITAT (United Nations Human Settlements Programme), UNIDO (United Nations Industrial Development Organisation), UNISDR (United Nations International

Strategy for Disaster Reduction) and the ILO did not meet these marketised development objectives, so DfID decided to withdraw core funding to established partners. Market-oriented judgements such as these are part of the wider strategy of securing the dominant status of neoliberalism as an expansive global framework for economic and social policy.

The 2010 Strategic Defence and Security Review (SDSR) made the commitment to deliver 30 per cent of overseas UK development spending specifically to fragile and conflict-affected states. The prioritisation of aid for fragile areas, the SDSR makes clear, is explicitly intended to manage the threat of terrorism and reduce future costs of intervention. In that context, in order to reach the 0.7 per cent target for aid, the UK coalition government ring-fenced aid spending from cuts to other public spending, which is an interesting choice when put into perspective: if the (DfID) had frozen funds at the same level they were in 2010–11, this capital could have been used to minimise real cuts to expenditure into the Department for Education by a third. Indeed, while the percentage of GNI used for overseas aid in conflict-driven areas will increase, spending will be focused on fewer countries and fewer issues, and will be channelled predominantly through the World Bank and the European Commission.

The ILO, one of the agencies cut from DfID's core funding roster, wrote an official response (ILO, 2011) the day after the Multilateral Aid Review was published, querying its methodology, noting that it was based on very limited research from only 33 projects in four countries. The Review thus cannot be generalised, and further, the ILO was shocked by these conclusions as they differed from the external evaluation issued by DfID itself only months previously, which looked favourably upon DfID's partnership with the ILO over the Partnership Framework Agreement (PFA) period 2006–09. The PFA concluded that partnership with the ILO should go on, and DfID should 'consider funding support to the ILO in the post-PFA period', and that in particular, the 'ILO's role and core mandate of promoting Decent Work is increasingly important'.

One trade union commentator believes that this clash is

> evidence that under the Conservatives, DfID is being transformed from a development body committed to lasting change in the global south into a sticking-plaster aid charity dispensing services to the poor to salve the conscience of the rich – as well as minimising the risk that the

poor will rise up and demand change more violently than we would like. (Tudor, 2011)

The Conservatives are not 'interested in the way the ILO combats poverty, which is to promote workers' rights – to join trade unions, to [promote] social security, and to [promote] decent work' (Tudor, 2011).

DfID overlooks social protection

Consciously applying a similar methodology to DfID's Review, the Trades Union Congress (TUC) launched a critique of DfID on the World Day for Decent Work, 7 October 2012, entitled 'A Decent Job? DfID and Decent Work'. The report claimed that DfID does not do enough to promote social dialogue, social protection, enable job creation and it has a low commitment to promotion of rights. TUC researchers read up-to-date annual reports and country implementation plans published in June 2012, and interviewed DfID staff to gather data about DfID's main bilateral projects. This was explicitly to identify whether DfID would fare well if held to account for a range of criteria in promoting decent work in the areas it invests.

The TUC gives DfID a score of six out of twelve in its ability to promote 'full and productive employment for all'. DfID, the TUC notes, has not made an explicit, public commitment to decent job creation nor any other indicator in the Decent Work Millennium Development Goal. Instead, DfID believes that 'promoting global prosperity is both a moral duty and in the UK's national interest. Aid is only ever a means to an end, never an end in itself. It is wealth creation and sustainable growth that will help people to lift themselves out of poverty' (DfID, 2012: 1). It does so by promoting a free trade area in Africa and a good climate for investment in businesses, as well as promotion of property rights and land. So DfID's commitment to decent work MDG targets is rated 1 out of 4, and the ideological divide could not be more overt. The TUC points out that there is little evidence that the activities around promoting financial opportunities for people in developing countries help to create decent jobs, nor to help people escape from poverty. Indeed, it is not clear that the microcredit and other financial programmes supported by DfID will work at all. Research supported by DfID itself oddly includes the comment that 'no clear evidence yet exists that microfinance programmes have positive impacts' (Duvendack, 2011, in TUC, 2012). Despite the fact that DfID prioritises the private sector as a tool and driver for growth, it rarely reports on the effectiveness of its projects. Given its own scathing report of the ILO's failure to report on progress, it is an odd oversight. Even on its own terms, TUC declares, DfID is weak, as it is not able to ensure a *responsible* private sector despite its support for the Fairtrade Foundation and the UN Global Compact, and it is given a 2 out of 4 rating. DfID also fails to require companies to adhere to environmental or social standards. Nonetheless, while increasing the percentage of GNI for international development aid, DfID stated its intention to support and fund projects in the private sector in developing states from 4.1 per cent to 8 per cent by 2014–15 (DfID, 2014).

The TUC report notes that DfID is happy to invest in strengthening government capacity toward business incentives and the private sector in developing areas, but it does not build scaffolding around labour standards. DfID aided Rwanda in reducing the registration process in setting up a business from nine days to two. However, in Bangladesh, workers who intend to claim unfair dismissal or other violations of rights wait for many years. The other misdemeanours include the failure to tackle workplace discrimination and child and forced labour.

TUC recommends promotion of decent work

TUC provides a set of clear recommendations that will help DfID promote decent work, and given the rise in social unrest in many of the areas DfID supports, it seems an obvious aim. As has been shown, international aid is now more than ever directly linked to security and cost cutting goals. Nonetheless, aid in conflict-affected areas continues to be exposed to risks of corruption and cannot ensure value for money, which is a paradox given the recent Multilateral Aid Review and the links between rising unemployment and rising social unrest and conflict in the Social Unrest Index (ILO, 2012). Given the link between unemployment and conflict, it is not clear why DfID would delegitimise organisations whose core focus is addressing unemployment issues, such as the ILO, and support the private sector almost exclusively in conflict riven areas without a clear agenda on social protection. The question is, if DfID does not advocate social protection in conflict areas but promotes development aid through relations with the private sector; and if the ILO is not supported in its social protection mandate and related projects; who will defend the employed and unemployed citizens in at-risk areas?

References

DfID (2011) 'Multilateral Aid Review: Ensuring Maximum Value for Money for UK Aid Through Multilateral Organisations'. Available from www.dfid.gov.uk.

DfID (2012) 'Operational Plan 2011–2015 DfID Private Sector Department'. Available from www.dfid.gov.uk.

DfID (2014) 'Department for International Development Annual Report and Accounts 2013–14'. Available from www.gov.uk/government/uploads/system/uploads/attachment_data/file/331591/annual-report-accounts-2013-14a.pdf.

ILO (2011) 'ILO Comments on UK Department for International Development Multilateral Aid Review'. Available from www.ilo.org.

ILO (2012) *World of Work Report 2012: Better jobs for a better economy*. Available from www.ilo.org.

Trade Unions Congress (TUC) (2012) A decent job? DfID and Decent Work. Available from www.tuc.org.uk.

Tudor, O. (2011) 'ILO cut is more than political bias: it's about ending a rights-based approach to poverty reduction' *Touchstone blog*. Available from http://touchstoneblog.org.uk.

22

The National Pact to Eradicate Slave Labour in Brazil: A Useful Tool for Unions?

Lisa Carstensen and Siobhán McGrath

In 2012 two major clothing retailers, the Spanish group Zara and the Brazilian Marisa, were suspended from membership of the Brazilian

'National Pact to Eradicate Slave Labour'. In both cases, the suspension occurred less than a year after the firms became members in the first place. As members of the Pact, they had pledged to eliminate slave labour from their supply chains. These cases generated a major debate – about forced labour in São Paulo's clothing industry but also about the Pact itself and about the 'Dirty List' of those found to be using slave labour.[1]

So how does the Pact work? Is it a model for other countries committed to the fight against forced labour? Is it useful for the trade union movement? What are its limitations? We argue that the Pact is a powerful tool which has been used to make progress in the ongoing fight against forced labour. It is necessary to provide first a short overview of the institutional and legal context of the Brazilian struggle against slave labour.

Why is there a Brazilian Pact to Eradicate Slave Labour?

The International Labour Organisation (ILO) Convention No. 29 defines forced labour as 'all work or service which is exacted from any person under the menace of any penalty and for which the said person has not offered (herself or) himself voluntarily'. Brazilian law prohibits 'reducing someone to conditions analogous to slavery'. Submitting someone to forced labour is explicitly defined as one means of doing so. While elements of coercion and/ or restricted mobility are common in cases of slave labour, the definition also comprises exhausting workdays and degrading working conditions as indicative. Throughout 2013 and 2014 there have been heated debates in the federal parliament and senate around the question whether degrading conditions alone qualify as slave labour. Both UN and ILO officials defended the broader Brazilian interpretation of the forced labour concept. In what follows we therefore use the term 'slave labour' when making reference to the specific Brazilian discussion.

Migrants in particular – mainly Brazilians who seek work within the country, but also transnational migrants – are sometimes trapped in debt or left without payment of wages. This may involve labour contractors, and/ or the truck system which obliges workers to purchase equipment and/or supplies at high prices directly from the employer. In some cases it may involve threats of physical harm by armed guards (Neide, 1994; Phillips

---

1. For a compilation of news reports see www.reporterbrasil.org.br/pacto/noticias.

and Sakamoto, 2012; Ricardo, 2004). Contemporary slave labour is mainly practised in rural economic activities such as cattle-ranching, extractive industries, charcoal and ethanol production (see Hervé et al., 2012). In these cases, slave labour may be found in relation to specific tasks such as cane cutting and forest clearing. Slave labour has also been observed in São Paulo's informal clothing industry where Latin American immigrants work and live in small sweatshops under extremely precarious conditions. Recently, slave labour has also been reported in the construction sector (Tanja and McGrath, 2011).

Responding to decades of activism and advocacy around the issue, the federal government, with support from the ILO, created the National Commission to Eradicate Slave Labour (CONATRAE) in 2003. The first and second National Plans for the Eradication of Forced Labour (2003 and 2008) designed a set of public policies including labour inspection through Special Mobile Inspection Groups, awareness campaigns aimed at prevention and labour market reintegration programmes.[2] As a result, the Ministry of Labour and Employment (MTE) reports than 46,478 workers were found and 'rescued' from forced labour between 1995 and 2013 (Ministério de Trabalho e Emprego, 2013).

As part of these efforts, the MTE also began compiling and publishing a 'Dirty List' of firms and individuals who have been found to use slave labour which is regularly updated and made available publicly (ILO, Ethos Institute and Repórter Brasil, 2011). Supported by the ILO, civil society organisations (Ethos Institute, Instituto Observatório Social and Repórter Brasil) launched the Pact in 2005 and formed the 'National Pact to Eradicate Slave Labour Institute' in 2014. Organisations and enterprises that form part of the Pact commit themselves to not collaborating with companies, farms or individuals named on the Dirty List (e.g., by using them as suppliers, or in the case of banks, extending credit). The National Pact is therefore a potentially powerful economic sanctioning mechanism. In order to identify labour rights infractions in the supply chains, a set of sectoral research projects was carried out by the non-governmental organisation Repórter Brasil. This organisation accompanies labour inspections and conducts independent research in order to provide and spread knowledge about slave

---

2. In 2014 the PEC 438/2001 do Trabalho Escravo was approved by the Brazilian Chamber of Deputies. This law would allow the expropriation of land without compensation in case of use of slave labour. However, it provoked a major debate on the legal definition of slave labour.

labour. Within the Pact research maps out the business links between the entities on the Dirty List and their buyers. On this basis signatory companies can be informed about their own links in the production networks. The voluntary use of the Dirty List works because enterprises are confronted with evidence of slave labour in their supply chains and the threat of going to the press. They are thus compelled to respond to such allegations.

Innovations, advances and limitations of the Pact

The Pact was launched in an effort to hurt employers economically and thereby make slave labour less profitable. Efforts to combat slave labour in Brazil had previously been plagued by issues of impunity and powerful resistance by the rural lobby. The Pact is a tool which can penalise companies that use slave labour more efficiently than the courts are able to. It is therefore not a 'solution' to this problem, but an innovative tool. Such tools are important. But of course, tools have to be used in order to have an impact. The Pact itself will not solve the problem, but it has been a resource for those trying to make a change.

As an instrument it should be understood in conjunction with overall labour market regulation and labour inspection. Fundamentally, the Pact has to be seen as an extension of the Dirty List. In contrast to other labour rights initiatives, state intervention in the form of a labour inspection typically serves as the catalyst for wider campaigns here. Some of these inspections may be triggered by action and complaints from workers and local activists – but not necessarily. Due to the nature of slave labour, the instrument tends to be used in situations where trade union activities are weak or non-existent and workers' organisational power is extremely low. Slave labour relations only become visible at the moment when they are denounced to authorities by either workers themselves, trade unions, the Catholic advocacy organisation, Pastoral Land Commission or migrant rights' organisations. During intervention, authorities usually 'liberate' or 'rescue' the workers and initiate legal action against the employer. In some cases action may also be taken against specific 'lead firms' in the production network, such as clothing retailers or pig iron plants, facilitated by regulations on subcontracting (*terceirização*) in which companies may be held partially responsible for labour conditions in cases where they outsource elements of their core business. In this regard, a limit to the National Pact is that it is to some extent reactive rather than pro-active.

Initially, companies can sign the agreement without taking on much responsibility. Often this only occurs after labour inspections discover slave labour. Once the agreement is signed the costs can become very high the moment that (further) problems are identified within the companies' supply chains. The Pact is innovative in its vision of shared responsibilities for labour rights violations, not only within companies but across the whole suppliers and outsourcing networks. It therefore goes beyond the national legislative framework and functions as a potentially transnational instrument which can strike at a company's key asset, its public image.

Smaller brands, however, are less vulnerable to attacks on their image, and in the case of São Paulo's garment industry, this appears to be a significant portion of the market. The semi-formal nature of the garment industry poses a further problem. Buyers may easily find another supplier not yet subject to labour inspections and the extent to which they carry out monitoring of their supply chains varies significantly by sector and by firm. More generally, the Dirty List itself is under constant legal challenge and many companies have managed to obtain injunctions preventing their names from appearing on it (see ILO, Ethos Institute and Repórter Brasil, 2005).

In this regard, the cases of the suspension of Zara and Marisa demonstrate the potential impact of the Pact. Both clothing retailers have been subject to scrutiny since suppliers were found using slave labour. As a response they legally challenged their inclusion on the Dirty List. In the case of Zara, the appeal against the inclusion in the dirty list was rejected in April 2014.

There is a broad consensus that slave labour is unacceptable, which provides legitimacy to the Pact. There is a flipside to this, however. The focus on the most extreme labour right violations risks isolating these from the wider struggles for decent work, the landscape of labour rights and the power relations which structure these. Therefore, in seeking to draw out lessons from Brazil, it is important to remember that a project like the Pact does not *automatically* strengthen workers' movements, trade unions or social movements. The Pact replaces the slow penal procedures and is able to exert pressure on transnational companies. But this does not *necessarily* improve workers' bargaining power in the respective sectors. In order to empower workers and translate this pressure into something more lasting, the struggles of social movements, trade unions and migrant organisations are crucial.

The Pact can of course provide a starting point for a more general debate about labour relations and regulations. Can the issue of slave labour be integrated into a broader struggle for decent work and its socio-political conditions? In the Brazilian case, social movements are recognising that slave labour needs to be tackled from multiple angles – the labour inspection model but also supply chains, migration and land reform. The annual immigrant march in São Paulo addressing topics such as 'Decent Work', 'Universal Citizenship' and 'Stop Violence against Immigrants' as well as the unification of organisations working towards land reform are emblematic of this continuing progress. Their strategy of embedding the struggle into a broader political context is something trade unions and social movements elsewhere can learn from.[3]

References

Hervé, T., Mello, N.A., Hato, J. and Girardi, E.P. (2012) 'Atlas do Trabalho Escravo no Brasil. Amigos da Terra – Amazônia Brasileira'. Available from http://amazonia.org.br.

ILO, Instituto Observatório Social, ONG Reporter Brasil, Instituto Ethos (2005) 'National Agreement to Eradicate Slave Labour'. Available at http://reporterbrasil.org.br/documentos/national_agreement.pdf.

Ministério de Trabalho e Emprego: Quadro geral das operações de fiscalização para erradicação do trabalho escravo. 2013. Available from http://portal.mte.gov.br.

Neide, E. (1994) Escravos da desigualdade: estudo sobre el uso represivo da forca de trabalho hoje (Rio de Janeiro: CEDI/ KOINONIA).

Phillips, N. and Sakamoto, L. (2012) 'Global Production Networks, Chronic Poverty and "Slave Labour" in Brazil', Studies in Comparative International Development, Vol. 47, No. 3.

Ricardo, R.F. (2004) Pisando fora da própria sombra: a escravidão por dívida no Brasil contemporâneo (Rio de Janeiro: Civilização Brasileira).

Tanja, B. and McGrath, S. (2011) 'Temporality, Migration and Unfree Labour: Migrant Garment Workers'. Available from http://tanjabastia.files.wordpress.com.

---

3. Visit the following mobilisation pages http://camimigrantes.com.br/site/ and http://encontrounitario.wordpress.com/declaracao-do-encontro/.

23

Better Work or 'Ethical Fix'?
Lessons from Cambodia's Apparel Industry

Dennis Arnold

The global apparel industry is characterised by low wages, poor occupational health and safety, and restrictions on freedom of association. These problems persist in spite of numerous corporate social responsibility initiatives, consumer campaigning for improved labour rights, and trade union organising in industrialising countries. In the wake of the Rana Plaza collapse in Bangladesh on 24 April 2013, debates over the 'race to the bottom' for cheap and flexible labour have re-emerged. For example, Disney corporate representatives, who terminated sourcing to Bangladesh in late 2012 in response to a spate of factory fires, were quoted in a recent article saying the company would consider allowing its licensees to produce in Bangladesh if the country implemented the International Labour Office (ILO)'s Better Work programme, which uses ILO monitoring of factories in Cambodia as its model (Greenhouse, 2013). Dan Rees, director of Better Work, is quoted in the same article saying that before his organisation would get involved in Bangladesh, the country needed to enact stronger labour protection and stop suppressing trade unions.

The seeds of the Better Work programme in Cambodia were planted in 1999, when the US and Cambodian governments initiated the three-year US–Cambodia Textile and Apparel Trade Agreement. It was extended for another three years, ending on the same day as the Multi Fibre Arrangement (MFA) phase-out on 31 December 2004 – the MFA consisted of non-tariff bilateral quotas established by developed countries to protect domestic industry. Along with the US–Cambodia Trade Agreement, an independent but complementary factory monitoring project, later named Better Factories Cambodia (BFC) was established in 2001 involving the ILO, the Cambodian government, garment manufacturers, and trade unions. The BFC's initial purpose was to inform US import quota allocation decisions.

If labour conditions in Cambodia's factories improved, the country would be granted increased US market access under the MFA. US market access was the carrot, and ILO monitoring the stick.

Initiatives stressing the importance of labour protection and trade union rights are a step in the right direction. Yet the Better Work's approach to such issues requires further examination. A joint programme of the ILO and the World Bank's International Finance Corporation (IFC), Better Work mediates global brand and retailers' needs to address reputation risk, with calls from labour activists for increased factory monitoring and space for workers to organise and join trade unions of their choosing. Cambodia is the programme's flagship. Based on experiences in Cambodia, Better Work is now also operating in Haiti, Indonesia, Jordan, Lesotho, Nicaragua and Vietnam, with plans to expand further in coming years. But how much 'better' is work in factories engaging in this programme? Has it actually empowered workers to achieve better wage and working conditions, or is it yet another high profile 'ethical fix' mechanism for brands to protect their images? Drawing on the Cambodia case, this article seeks to answer these questions. After an overview of recent debate on the BFC programme, the article looks at structural factors delimiting workers' potential to negotiate a living wage in Cambodia. The article concludes that the efforts should be geared towards redistributing wealth and power in favour of workers.

A carrot but no stick

The BFC programme has been much lauded, but since the end of global MFA quotas under the WTO in 2005, serious cracks have emerged in the system. Research has shown that the ILO has lost its power of enforcement with the elimination of global quotas (Arnold and Toh Han, 2010). Increased US market access drove many of the factory level improvements associated with the early years of the project. As Jill Tucker, BFC's chief technical advisor declared:

> At present, BFC monitors all garment export factories but has no enforcement powers to address violations. Where it is our role to identify the areas of non-compliance, the power to directly enact changes lies with buyers and factories. BFC's presence has assisted in many positive

developments in Cambodia's garment industry [but] we do not have any influence over issues that buyers and factories do not prioritise. (Quoted in Janssens, 2013)

Lacking power of enforcement, BFC has been criticised for playing into global retailers and brands desire to protect their image, while the ILO and World Bank continue to promote it as a model of decent work in global supply chains. Sourcing in Cambodia has been used as a 'showcase' for corporations' ethical commitment. Is the model as effective as these players claim?

Structural factors and (dis)empowered workers

Cambodia's garment and shoe factories have become notorious for mass fainting; over 4,000 workers have fainted at work over the past two years. Fainting is attributed to numerous factors, with overwork and malnourishment or undernourishment commonly cited by ILO researchers and Cambodian NGOs and trade unions. An underlying factor is that real wages have *decreased* over the past decade, due to rising costs in Cambodia, forcing workers into excessive overtime shifts. In the meantime, global brands and retailers have kept a safe distance from wage negotiations in Cambodia, claiming they are a matter of national interest. In Cambodia a tripartite body, the Labour Advisory Committee, meets on an ad hoc basis to determine wage increases. The Committee comprises a state that has consolidated political power through 'electoral authoritarianism', and an employers association that is openly hostile to both independent trade unions and the BFC programme.

Cambodian garment workers' power to negotiate a decent wage and other critical issues is closely related to the balance of forces between these stakeholders. BFC is peripheral to wage negotiations because these are outside of its mandate; the buyers engaging in the programme are further removed from workers' wage concerns. The institutional overcrowding of garment trade unions in Cambodia, one result of the US–Cambodia Trade Agreement that created space for plant-level unions by compelling factories to take part in factory monitoring (Arnold and Toh Han, 2010), further complicates national level tripartite negotiations. Despite exceptionally high unionisation rates in Cambodia's garment industry, standing at roughly 60 per cent, an average of 1.7 trade unions per factory, with 88 garment trade union federations in the country, workers have limited ability to promote their interests. Independent trade (pro-worker) unions contend that this can be attributed to workers' precarious position vis-à-vis employers, the state and even most trade unions – a majority of which are controlled by the ruling Cambodian People's Party (CPP), employers, or are 'entrepreneurial organisations' seeking kickbacks from employers (Arnold, 2014).

Cambodia has an institutional overcrowding of unions, combined with the decoupling of an international CSR paradigm of labour rights monitoring from workers' and independent unions' interests. This constellation of relations is embedded in a country experiencing rapid economic growth marked by increasing inequality and instability generated by regional economic dynamics driven by highly volatile garment production for global markets. For example, employment in garment and shoe manufacturing has fluctuated from 350,000 in 2008, to 297,000 in 2009, up to roughly 400,000 in 2013. These structural forces tightly delineate workers' agency. Workers' response to this configuration is marked by increasingly frequent strikes, many of which are led by 'real' unions, indicating that despite numerous obstacles, the ability to undertake industrial actions has emerged. The number of strikes in 2012 nearly quadrupled from 2011, to 134. Labour unrest, combined with regular images in the media of fainting factory workers, has generated much attention in recent national elections.

In May 2013 the monthly minimum wage increased from $61 to $75 per month, well short of a 'survival wage' of $100. Garment workers' concerns has been a key campaign point for the opposition Cambodia National Rescue Party in the lead up to the July 2013 elections – with opposition leader Sam Rainsy promising a $150 per month minimum wage if elected. In response to garment workers' support for the opposition, on 26 August the ruling CPP promised to revisit wage negotiations by 2014. Thus, it is a critical juncture for garment workers and trade unions to use their leverage as a voting bloc to pressure both parties in government to deliver on calls for better wages. Better Work could make a significant contribution by seeking apparel buyers' commitments that a decent wage would not induce capital flight – a longstanding concern of the Cambodian government that views cheap labour as its competitive advantage in the Asia regional division of labour.

The BFC initiative has become nonbinding and unenforceable. With MFA quota phase out in 2005 corporate enforcement of monitoring has become voluntary, further diffusing brand and retailer responsibility to ensure a living wage and decent work in supply chains. Despite the fanfare surrounding the BFC, workers have gained little at a time when the 'Cambodia model' has gone global under the Better Work banner. By implementing non-binding programmes that offer carrots without wielding a stick, poverty wages and precarious work continue to be the norm in Cambodia's garment factories. This has generated widespread protests. Needed are binding mechanisms that contribute to empowering workers with independent unions utilising their collective labour power to negotiate living wages. Such efforts can be effective if situated in broader efforts to redistribute wealth and power in favour of workers – rather than create new forms of dependency by privileging image risk mitigation as a primary mechanism to deliver on workers' rights.

References

Arnold, D. (2014) 'Workers' Agency and Power Relations in Cambodia's Garment Industry', in Luinstra, A., Pickles, J. and Rossi, A. (eds) *Toward Better Work: Understanding Labour in Global Supply Chains* (London and Geneva: Palgrave Macmillan and International Labour Organisation).

Arnold, D. and Toh Han, S. (2010) 'A Fair Model of Globalisation? Labour and Global Production in Cambodia', *Journal of Contemporary Asia*, Vol. 40, No. 3.

Greenhouse, S. (2013) 'Some Retailers Rethink Role in Bangladesh', *New York Times*. Available from www.nytimes.com.

Janssens, F. (2013) 'Monitoring for Nothing', *Southeast Asia Globe*. Available from http://sea-globe.com.

24

Putting Workers' Agency at the Centre in the Indonesian Sportswear Industry[4]

Karin A. Siegmann, Jeroen Merk and Peter Knorringa

Globalisation of production has been accompanied by a rise of informal and insecure work across different regions of the world, even in formal establishments. Yet, the role of labour has received scant attention in both the governance and analyses of global production networks (GPNs). Therefore, activists and scholars have demanded a 'sea-change in the international business model and the active participation of informed and empowered workers' (Brown, 2013: 5) that needs to be flanked by an analytical framework that puts workers' agency at the centre.

This has motivated us to analyse the Freedom of Association Protocol, a voluntary initiative (VI) that has been implemented in the Indonesian sportswear industry since 2011. In that year, Indonesian exports of leather and leather goods peaked, generating more than US$230 million in revenues (Statistics Indonesia, 2014). Overall, more than 600,000 workers were employed in the footwear industry in the same year, including production for the domestic market (CCC, 2014). In export factories manufacturing footwear for Nike alone, one of the largest foreign buyers, more than 170,000 workers are currently employed, the vast majority of which are women workers (Nike, 2014).

From the perspective of Wright's (2000) theory of the factors enabling positive class compromise, we have asked under which conditions VIs with a more active role for labour can emerge. Wright defines positive class compromise as 'mutual cooperation between opposing classes'. It involves concessions in favour of the interests of people in the opposing class. His central argument is that the possibilities for stable, positive class compromise hinge on the relationship between the strength of workers' organisations

---

4. A longer version of this chapter was published as an ISS working paper: http://repub.
    eur.nl/pub/51297/

(that is, 'associational power') and their ability to help capitalists to solve collective action and coordination problems.

Freedom of association (FoA) and collective bargaining (CB) are often referred to as 'enabling rights', implying that, when these rights are respected, workers can use them to ensure that other labour standards are upheld. While they often formally acknowledge the relevance of FoA and CB, VIs in labour-intensive sectors such as the sportswear industry have a notoriously poor record of implementing and monitoring these collective labour rights. We consider the Indonesian FoA Protocol a far-going structural commitment to strengthening labour. Its study might therefore contain lessons for forms of non-governmental labour regulation that are less far-going in their concessions in favour of labour.

Workers' struggles in Indonesia and the emergence of an alternative model

All main producer countries for athletic sportswear, namely China and Vietnam alongside Indonesia, have a history of severely curtailed collective labour rights. Both in China and Vietnam, workers are legally restricted to form independent unions. In Indonesia, the Suharto regime (1967–98) strongly restricted trade union activity and the employee's voice in the workplace. This regularly included army intervention in the case of workers struggles.

These struggles nonetheless had an impact beyond the local and national level when Western media began to cover these events, highlighting sweatshop conditions at famous brands like Nike or Adidas. During the 1990s, the contacts between Indonesian labour NGOs and transnational anti-sweatshop networks such as Oxfam Australia, the European-based Clean Clothes Campaigns (CCC), the US-American United Students Against Sweatshop (USAS), the International Textile Garment, Leather Workers Federation (ITGLWF, now IndustriALL) and others became more intense. This international collaboration was continued in the post-Suharto era, for instance in the Play Fair campaign. Launched in connection with the 2004 Olympic Games held in Athens, this cross-border alliance sought to push sportswear and athletic footwear companies, the International Olympics Committee and its national organising committees, as well as national governments to take concrete measures to address violations of workers' rights in supply chains.

The end of the Suharto regime removed earlier restrictions on trade union establishment, leading to a steep rise in the number of trade unions. Yet, these political and legal changes did not end the violence, intimidation and the imprisonment of outspoken workers or union officials. Despite continued repression, Indonesian trade unions are among the most militant in the region. Therefore, workers' struggles often escalate even before an attempt at finding a resolution can be mounted in the context of existing VIs. The FoA Protocol described below addresses this situation by paving the way for a more effective guarantee of collective labour rights at the firm level.

On 6 June 2011, Indonesian trade unions, large Indonesian sportswear manufacturers and multinational sportswear brands, including Adidas, Nike, Puma, Pentland, New Balance, and Asics signed a protocol on FoA. The ratification was one of the results of sportswear campaigns around the 2008 Beijing Olympic Games. The Protocol stands out for two reasons: firstly, it involved both direct employers and 'indirect' employers, that is, the brands that have a powerful role in these production networks; and, secondly, the process was driven by Indonesian union federations instead of being imposed upon them as in most VIs.

The resulting Protocol establishes practical guidelines for how to ensure that factory workers in Indonesia are able to organise and collectively bargain for better conditions in their workplaces. The agreement also covers areas concerning non-victimisation of trade union officers and members as well as a non-intervention pledge on the part of employers into trade union activities. In addition, the Protocol describes in much more detail than the national law (let alone, multinational brands' VIs) what rights unions can claim at the factory level. This includes for example the right to have an on-site union office, to publicise materials, to access workers etc. Indonesian union representatives find the Protocol to be more detailed than the law, giving more space for workers to organise as a result.

The FoA Protocol: putting workers' agency at the centre

While it is too early to assess the effectiveness of the FoA Protocol, against the backdrop of union oppression in Indonesia's export industries, its ratification as such is a significant achievement. Yet, it raises the question why capitalists would submit to the unattractive option of structural collaboration with labour through a VI?

Indonesian workers' associational power was enhanced through transnational labour solidarity networks, yet, five local unions were at the forefront of the negotiations for the FoA Protocol. This is reflected in the Protocol's stipulations, which cater to the practical needs of local unions rather than referring to abstract principles. The coordination on the labour side increased pressure on producers and brands, who had a less united and clear agenda, but also allowed them to solve their respective collective action problems. This included addressing producers' concerns regarding the choking of production through fierce labour struggles. The Protocol also ensures that defecting producers do not achieve competitive advantage at the expense of collective labour rights. For sportswear brands, the Protocol offers a unique opportunity to protect and increase their reputation as a business community that is 'playing fair' with regards to collective labour rights. Overall, it allows actors in the athletic footwear industry in Indonesia to move from a situation of confrontation to one that has the potential to catalyse cooperation and benefit workers.

Critical question marks are also due. First, we have concentrated on the question of which factors have catalysed the emergence of the FoA Protocol as a VI with the potential to create spaces for workers' collective agency. Yet, the actual *impact* on guaranteeing Indonesian sportswear workers' collective rights will be the litmus test for the Protocol's effectiveness. Secondly, we have implicitly defined workers in the Indonesian athletic sportswear industry as those directly employed in manufacturers' plants. A significant number of workers are employed in second-tier suppliers, though. Despite trade unions' and their partners' attempts to extend the coverage of the Protocol to second tier producers, these efforts were met with resistance from brands. Hence, even if effective for directly employed workers, one may question whether this VI can be seen as truly contributing to strengthening labour. Thirdly, the sphere of politics may deserve more attention. Which role did the Indonesian political class play in the emergence of the Protocol? While the ratification of the FoA Protocol can be seen as signalling a move towards a greater degree of enforceability of the VI and inclusiveness regarding the actors involved, there is so far no evidence of a greater commitment of the Indonesian state to enforce legally guaranteed collective labour rights.

Overall, we conclude that while the spatial dispersion of production has weakened state mechanisms for the guarantee of labour rights, new pressure points for labour have also emerged, such as brands' reputation or just-in-time production. Besides, new possibilities for transnational labour networks have opened that strengthen workers' associational power. Moreover, GPNs fragment capital in different factions, such as producers and brands. Their material concerns are not necessarily the same. Workers' movements might be able to benefit from such divergent interests, especially if they are in a position to help solving producers and buyers' collective action problems. We conclude that if VIs are to create conditions under which decent work can be strengthened, the involvement and strength of local labour organisations is required and producers' and/or buyers' dependence on workers' cooperation may act as a catalyst.

References

Brown, G. (2013) 'The Record of Failure and Fatal Flaws of CSR Factory Monitoring', *ISHN Journal*, 1–6. Available from http://mhssn.igc.org.

Clean Clothes Campaign (CCC) (2014) 'Indonesia: Living Wage', draft research on file.

Nike (2014) 'Global Manufacturing'. Available from http://manufacturingmap. nikeinc.com.

Statistics Indonesia (2014) *Economic Indicators* (Jakarta: Statistics Indonesia).

Wright, E.O. (2000) 'Working-Class Power, Capitalist-Class Interests, and Class Compromise', *American Journal of Sociology*, Vol. 105, No. 4.

25

Rana Plaza: Private Governance and Corporate Power in Global Supply Chains

Tandiwe Gross

With a death toll of over 1,120 people and more than 2,500 people injured, the collapse of the Rana Plaza building in Bangladesh in 2013 is one of the worst industrial accidents in world history. Besides shops and a bank, the building accommodated five garment factories with more than 3,000 workers. A day prior to the accident, workers identified major cracks in the building, which prompted a police evacuation order. Despite this, on 24 April 2013 the workers were forced by management to enter the building. The garment factories in Rana Plaza supplied to a number of popular international brands, including Primark, Le Bon Marché, Joe Fresh, El Corte Ingles, KiK and Mango. Fatal accidents are nothing new in the country's garment industry: even before Rana Plaza, more than 700 workers have died in the industry since 2005 (International Labour Rights Forum, 2012). Only a few months prior to Rana Plaza, 112 workers died in a fire at the Tazreen Fashion factory in Dhaka. More than eight years after the infamous Spectrum factory collapse, Rana Plaza has shown that the structural causes of unsafe working conditions in Bangladesh's garment industry have not changed.

The Bangladeshi garment industry: unequal power relations between capital and labour

Due to its low labour costs, Bangladesh has become the second largest exporter of garments, after China. Constituting 17 per cent of the country's gross national product and 78 per cent of its exports, the garment industry is the backbone of the national economy. The sector employs around three million – mostly female – workers at wages which are the lowest in the world in relation to other garment workers. Over the last years, garment factories have been mushrooming around the country; they are often set up in residential buildings which do not meet the necessary safety requirements for industrial production. Despite a major labour law reform in 2006 which brought a few improvements in health and safety regulations, labour inspection is extremely weak. According to the Bangladesh Occupational Safety, Health and Environment Foundation, only 20 government inspectors were responsible for monitoring occupational health and safety in around three million small-scale establishments and more than 24,000 registered factories in 2008. Furthermore, substantial barriers to union formation remain even after the reform: a union requires a 30 per cent membership in a factory in order to be registered and employers have to be provided with a list of union officers applying for registration (International Trade Union Confederation, 2012).

While the more than 370,000 workers employed in 'Special Economic Zones' have long been legally barred from forming unions, a reform proposed in 2014 allows for the registration of 'associations'.

Trade union organising is extremely difficult as workers and union activists are subject to a high degree of both state and management repression, ranging from false criminal charges against union leaders to cases of torturing and murdering of union activists, such as the murder of garment labour rights activist Aminul Islam in 2012. After a short flourishing of the trade union movement after 1971 under state-led industrialisation, the strength of organised labour gradually declined after 1973 with the introduction of free-market policies. These pressures were exacerbated by internal divisions along political party lines, leading to a highly fragmented trade union movement. Overall union density stood at less than 3 per cent in 2002 (Mondol, 2002). With organised labour playing a limited role, garment workers started to organise in the early 1990s mainly in the form of spontaneous, self-organised protests (Khanna, 2011). Today, garment workers are represented by four main union federations at the national level, while union density in the sector is as low as 5 per cent (Miller, 2012).

Despite severe repression from the state and management, garment workers have become increasingly assertive in the struggle for their rights as illustrated by the regular outbursts of often militant labour unrest over the last years. However, while workers' resistance is growing, the unequal power relations between capital and labour are intensified by a strong collusion between garment manufacturers and the state: more than 10 per cent of the current parliament seats in Bangladesh are occupied by owners of garment factories who have repeatedly blocked initiatives for stricter regulations (Al-Mahmood and Wright, 2013).

The power of transnational capital in the global garment supply chain

The dominance of capital at the local level is compounded by the massive power of transnational corporations at the global level: characterised by a small number of powerful international buyers and a large number of fragmented suppliers in 'developing' countries, the global garment industry is a typical example of a 'buyer-driven' supply chain (Gereffi, 1994).

Over the last decades, international buyers sourcing from Bangladesh have developed various factory audit systems as part of voluntary corporate social responsibility (CSR). In this system of private corporate governance, companies are able to define unilaterally which standards they set and how compliance is being controlled. Relying on audits by external auditing firms, these systems have been widely criticised by civil society organisations for excluding local trade unions and having minimal oversight over the factories. Indeed, two of the factories in the collapsed Rana Plaza building had been certified as being compliant with the standards of the Business Social Compliance Initiative (BSCI), a company-controlled CSR initiative with over 1,000 member companies in Europe. Similarly, the garment factory Ali Enterprises in Pakistan, which burned down on 11 September 2012 killing more than 262 workers, had been certified by the international auditing organisation Social Accountability International (SAI) less than a month before the fire. In that sense, the tragedy of Rana Plaza has once again revealed the fundamental failure of the private code of conduct and auditing system. Instead of empowering labour on the ground it rather serves as a means to 'replace' trade union organising by suggesting that workers' interests are sufficiently protected by external auditors. Furthermore, due to the buyer-driven nature of the global garment supply chain, transnational corporations are able to exert massive price and delivery pressures on their suppliers. These pressures leave suppliers with very little space for implementing safe and decent working conditions and create incentives to suppress trade union organising in order to keep production running and labour costs low.

From private governance to binding accountability and priority of trade union rights

In response to a large amount of international pressure, more than 60 international brands and retailers have now signed the Bangladesh Fire and Building Safety Agreement, a multi-stakeholder agreement between the signatory brands and a coalition of local trade unions and labour organisations, global unions and international labour rights campaigns. It includes a two-year programme with independent inspections of buildings and publication of results, access of trade unions to the factories, disclosure of the names of suppliers, and creation of worker-led factory health and safety committees. Set up as a legally binding agreement which assigns a central role to local trade unions, it represents a major step towards a more accountable and worker-oriented approach to improving the situation in the sector. However, the agreement is largely limited to direct suppliers of buyers, it only covers the garment industry of Bangladesh and it is confined to questions of health and safety while omitting structural exploitation through excessive working hours, poverty wages and harassment of workers.

The dominant system of private, voluntary governance of working conditions in global supply chains needs to be questioned in a fundamental way. Looking back on the results of two decades of voluntary CSR, it can be expected that without binding accountability rules for transnational corporations which prioritise trade union rights and address price and delivery pressures in the global supply chain, concerns of cheap in-time production will continue to dominate over concerns of decent working conditions.

The European Coalition for Corporate Justice (2010) therefore suggests a framework of binding corporate accountability via mandatory annual social and environmental reporting, a liability of parent companies for human rights and environmental abuses of both subsidiaries and suppliers, and access of victims of corporate human rights violations to EU courts.

While, on a systemic level, only a departure from an economic system which treats labour as a mere 'cost factor' will bring about real change, binding accountability of corporations and prioritising trade union rights on the ground are important steps towards improving the situation of workers in global supply chains. Here, both the Bangladesh Fire and Building Safety Agreement and the accountability framework outlined above may be seen as a chance to build momentum for shifting away from the unregulated private governance system of global supply chains.

References

Al-Mahmoud, S.Z. and Wright, T. (2013) 'Collapsed Factory Was Built Without Permit', *Wall Street Journal*, 26 April. Available from http://online.wsj.com.
European Coalition for Corporate Justice (2010) *Principles and Pathways: Legal Opportunities to Improve Europe's Corporate Accountability Framework* (Brussels).

Gereffi, G. (1994) 'The organisation of buyer-driven global commodity chains', in Gereffi, G. and Korzeniewicz, M. (eds) *Commodity Chains and Global Capitalism* (Westport, CT: Greenwood Press).

International Labour Rights Forum (2012) *New Report documents Fire Safety Cover-Ups by US retailers*. Available from http://laborrights.org.

International Trade Union Confederation (2012) *Internationally Recognised Core Labour Standards in Bangladesh*, Report for the WTO General Council Review of the Trade Policies of Bangladesh, 24–26 September 2012. Available from www.ituc-csi.org.

Khanna, P. (2011) 'Making Labour Voices Heard During an Industrial Crisis: Workers' struggles in the Bangladesh garment industry', *Labour, Capital and Society*, Vol. 44, No. 2.

Miller, D. (2012) *Last Nightshift in Savar: The Story of the Spectrum Sweater Factory Collapse* (Alnwick: McNidder & Grace).

Mondol, A.H. (2002) 'Globalisation, Industrial Relations and Labour Policies: The Need for Renewed Agenda', in Muqtada, M., Singh, A.M. and Rashid, M.A. (eds) *Bangladesh: Economic and Social Challenges of Globalisation* (Geneva and Dhaka: International Labour Organisation and University Press).

'Workers of the World, Unite': Challenges and Opportunities of Transnational Solidarity

26

Rank and File Participation and International Union Democracy

Vasco Pedrina

Trade union democracy and active rank and file participation are two sides of the same coin, both nationally and internationally. Historically, trade unions were built and operated almost exclusively by workers who devoted their spare time to the union cause. Along with the growth in their membership and the development of their economic strength, trade unions developed administrative and technical structures whose operation has increasingly been ensured by full-time union officials. Ultimately, this organisational transformation often led to bureaucracy, and the weakening of rank and file participation and trade union democracy. This transformation was characterised by an ever-increasing delegation of tasks from the active union base to the full-time union officials, a shift in union activities from the field to trade union offices, and a weaker trade union presence in the workplace.

From trade unionism in a booming economy to trade unionism in hard times

During the economic boom of the '30 glorious years' (or Golden Age) that followed the Second World War, the impact of these developments was not very serious for the workers in countries with strong trade union traditions (Pedrina, 2008). For workers in such countries it was not too difficult to negotiate socially progressive agreements with employers or the state at the bargaining table. Born from the ashes of a terrible war, the 'Spirit of Philadelphia', which gave rise to the 'European Social Model', provided the guiding framework for the relatively calm labour relations characteristic of the period, at least in developed countries (Supiot, 2010). The neoliberal offensive of the 1980s and 1990s, together with the first serious signs of systemic crisis, radically changed the situation. Many unions found themselves paralysed by their bureaucracies, powerless in the face of the trends evolving in the consumer society, and confronted by a new generation of US-style managers and hard-right politicians who had no time for social dialogue. In short, trade unions were no longer being taken seriously as a countervailing power.

For union leaders who took leadership in the early 1990s, the question became, and remains, how to ensure that trade unions would regain strength and respect from employers and politicians in social and political matters. The Swiss response from both the inter-industrial union Unia and the USS (Swiss Trade Union Confederation) has had some success with its political-organisational approach to this challenge, aiming at two objectives.

First, professionalising trade union operations by applying modern NGO management methods, with the dual objective of improving benefits/services to individual members and raising the effectiveness of invested resources so as to release additional resources for the real work of building up trade unionism, especially in the 'trade union deserts' of the private services sector and female-dominated sectors.

Secondly, reactivating the trade union base by (re)gaining a presence in workplaces, with the aim of creating a new generation of committed and combative activists.

A critical question arose, however: how does one reconcile the two approaches of professionalisation and participation, which at first appear contradictory? Indeed, professionalisation of union structures requires management to be based on clearly hierarchical rules, as in any enterprise, whereas active participation of the rank and file cannot flourish in a strongly hierarchical context, but only in a strongly democratic one.

Our experience in the restructuring of the Swiss trade union movement shows that this is not only possible, but even that such an approach – carried out consistently and systematically – is a condition for the revival of a combative and attractive trade union movement.

From a trade union of full-time officials to a trade union of activists

To become a trade union movement that is capable of responding to the challenges of the neoliberal dogma, of defending itself against social demolition, and instigating real societal change, our active trade union bases must take charge of their organisations' destiny, conferring upon the full-time union officials the roles of coach and back-up in trade union struggles.

It is with that line of thinking that in 2008 we launched a new project to transform the organisation, under the banner of 'Unia Forte'. We condensed this new challenge in the formula: 'From a trade union of full-time union officials to one of activists.' A second slogan guiding us is: 'Promote rank and file-based democracy, not apparatus-led "substitution unionism".' We envision a trade union that knows how to combine its role of being a combative social movement with that of a highly professional non-profit services organisation. Box 26.1 outlines the full list of objectives.

Achieving this vision presupposes profound cultural change in the entire organisation, in its functioning and in its practices. Needless to say, cultural change is very difficult for a trade union organisation to achieve. The paternalistic (and frequently manipulative) style of behaviour of the union apparatus towards the active base must give way to a practice where the full-time union officials act as coaches to activists and unionised workers, promoting their empowerment and their willingness to accept responsibilities in union activities. This cultural change is also needed within the rank and file, who have to demand more from union officials; especially when there is a need to show courage, namely during concerted trade union action. It requires new training concepts, great perseverance, and continuity.

. . . with exemplary trade union officials in their role as coaches

The process of political-organisational transformation forces new questions and critical discussions. One worthy of mention is the 'self-awareness' of the full-time union officials. It is clear that a re-orientation of the trade union movement to become a force that is credible and trustworthy, independent from political parties and from employers, with a combative spirit, and embodying guiding principles for another society based on equality and social justice presupposes having full-time union officials who meet high moral integrity requirements, who see their occupation as a vocation, act as coaches for active workers, and exemplify our values (equality, solidarity, social justice, democracy, peace, sustainability). At the same time, the model of the generalist trade union secretary must give way to more

Box 26.1   Unia Forte (= a strong Unia)

1. General objectives of action with the activists

A. Primary objective – Vision

In the trade union Unia, the activists active in enterprises, industries, social and political movements, and in trade union bodies fight for social justice. They are supported by committed trade union officials.

B. Strategic objectives – Organisation

- Unia is an effective force in the workplace, able to rely on activists ready to act, who organise themselves collectively and are capable of conducting concerted action and of defending Unia's values and objectives in the workplace. The activists also organise their fellow workers in the enterprise.
- In industries and sectors, the activists delegated by local activists' groups decide industrial and sectoral policies.
- Trade union campaigns are jointly developed and carried out by activists and trade union officials.
- Unia bodies (local groups, sections, regions, national bodies) are directed by elected and competent activists.

C. Strategic objectives – Activists

The activists have the necessary motivation and capacities to exercise their functions.

2. Specific Objectives 2013–16

- Strengthening the network of activists is an integral part of each activity, campaign, meeting.
- Close to 3,000 new activists and supporters are involved with the trade union officials in organising trade union actions.
- There is a specific training programme for activists; for trade union officials, there is support in working with activists.
- Developing groups: there are functional groups at least in the largest firms. There are industrial groups in the regions/sections. The national industrial delegates are elected by the local groups.
- Specific measures aimed at activating the growing female membership are created. These must take into consideration their particular situation and often existing double burden.
- Activists participate in member recruitment.

differentiated models, taking into account both the evolution of society and the specialisation needs of trade union organisations facing increasingly complex demands.

An internationalist spirit and practice as levers for the revival of a democratic and combative trade union movement

The integration of the internationalist perspective into the trade union revitalisation movement means approaching the subject in terms of both national and global unions – even the anti-globalisation social movements.

Starting from the belief, based on historical experience, that genuine and positive trade unionism cannot be anything but internationalist – especially in an era of capitalist globalisation and with the growing importance of regional or continental inter-governmental organisations – the question for each national trade union is how to promote within its ranks an internationalist spirit and practice. This question is especially relevant in Europe, since, following the international financial crisis 2007/08 and the long euro crisis, one is compelled to note a 'national retreat and isolationism' among unions. This is particularly worrying in the political context of a surge in the populist and nationalist forces of a profoundly anti-union extreme right. Those trends can be countered only by trade union leaders who work to promote:

- Cross-border actions targeting multinational companies and industries.
- Cooperation projects and international solidarity campaigns, in which the union rank and file are actively involved, such as in the construction industry's 'Fair Games – Fair Play' campaign for the FIFA (Football) World Cup 2010 (South Africa), 2014 (Brazil) and 2022 (Qatar).
- Opportunities for exchange of experiences and training (through European Works Councils or trade union networks in multinational companies).
- Alliances with the social movements of civil society that fight for another world!

To fulfil their role to promote strong and combative trade unionism based on an active trade union base, global unions should follow a 'debureaucratisation' process to redirect resources towards the exchange of 'best practices' and initiatives that have the potential to move the entire trade union movement in the right direction, namely towards internationalist trade unionism capable of contributing to the necessary change of course towards a societal alternative to the permanent threat of social barbarism.

References

Pedrina, V. (2008) 'Member Recruitment and Organising – Rules for the Trade Union of the Future and New Approaches to Trade Union Organising in Europe', *Organising in the Building and Wood Industries* (Building & Wood Workers' International – BWI).

Supiot, A. (2010) 'A legal perspective on the economic crisis of 2008', *International Labour Review*, Vol. 149, No. 6.

27

Trade Unions, Free Trade and the Problem of Transnational Solidarity

Andreas Bieler

Tensions between European trade unions and unions from the global South over international free trade developed into an open confrontation during the talks over the revival of the World Trade Organisation (WTO) Doha round in 2008. The European Metal Workers' Federation (EMF) joined forces with the European Automobile Manufacturers' Association (ACEA) in the publication of two joint press releases demanding reciprocal market access in developed, emerging and developing countries. This led to an angry response by trade unions in the global South, especially the

Confederation of South African Trade Unions (Cosatu). The EMF was accused of undermining workers' solidarity, since their cooperation with European employers in demanding equal market access would imply job losses in the South and undermine the internal unity of the International Trade Union Confederation (ITUC) (Bieler, 2013).

The WTO Doha negotiations have stalled for years. And yet, free trade agreements (FTAs) continue to be pushed in bilateral negotiations by the US and the EU with developing countries and emerging markets. The negotiations of a Transatlantic Trade and Investment Partnership between the EU and US as well as the Transpacific Partnership Agreement are only the latest initiatives in this respect. Importantly, these FTAs no longer only concern trade in manufactured goods, but now also include issues of intellectual property rights, trade in services and investment as well as the highly controversial investor-state dispute settlement instrument (Hilary, 2014). Unsurprisingly, the tensions within the international labour movement persist (Bieler et al., 2014). In this chapter, I will discuss the obstacles but also possibilities for establishing transnational solidarity in relation to tensions over trade liberalisation.

Liberal economic theory and developmental reality

In order to understand such tensions over free trade policies, the historical dynamics of capitalist accumulation need to be conceptualised. In a liberal understanding of capitalist development, free trade is regarded as a win-win situation, a positive-sum game. As David Ricardo famously argued, if every country concentrates on producing and exporting what it is best at, i.e. on its comparative advantage, and imports all the other necessities, everybody would benefit as a result. Neoliberal economic thinking about the extension of free trade in times of globalisation builds on this understanding. States should refrain from intervening in the economy and instead deregulate and liberalise markets, including the labour market, in order to facilitate free trade. If developing countries open up to free trade and foreign direct investment, development would follow and allow them to catch up with developed countries.

However, the false promises of liberal economic thinking have been exposed. In a study by the non-governmental organisation (NGO) War on Want, it is illustrated that global economic growth in the 1980s and 1990s, the time of neoliberal globalisation, was slower than in the 1960s and 1970s. Moreover, 'the number of people unemployed and the number in unstable, insecure jobs has actually increased – from 141 million to 190 million (1993 to 2007) and from 1.338 million to 1.485 million (1997 to 2007) respectively' (War on Want, 2009: 4). Developing countries have been the main losers of this period. Trade liberalisation often implied de-industrialisation and import dependence for them. Workers in industrialised countries have been predominantly employed in high value-added, high productivity production processes. Moreover, from 1945 onwards they have made significant achievements within national social pacts. In exchange for accepting capital's prerogative over the organisation of the work process and the private ownership of the means of production, they were allowed to participate in increasing profits through rising wages and expansive welfare states. Increasing exports through FTAs implied directly secure jobs and higher wealth levels for workers. In contrast, workers in the global South have not experienced these positive dynamics. They have mainly been integrated into the global economy as exporters of agricultural goods and raw materials. Where there has been a diffusion of manufacturing especially since the 1970s, it has often been in the area of labour-intensive industries characterised by low productivity. Even China, often hailed as a success story of development by liberals, continues to rely on its vast army of cheap labour in order to remain competitive.

At the global level, free trade links countries in the core, which export high productivity/high value-added goods (and increasingly services), with countries in the periphery, the exports of which are based on low productivity. As Ernest Mandel argued, 'on the world market, the labour of a country with a higher productivity of labour is valued as more intensive, so that the product of one day's work in such a nation is exchanged for the product of more than a day's work in an underdeveloped country' (Mandel, 1975: 71–2). Hence, countries in the periphery have become locked into relations of unequal exchange in which surplus value is transferred from the periphery to the core. This has resulted in an intensified polarisation and inequality between countries in the core and countries in the periphery. In short, capitalist development has been highly uneven and so-called 'free trade' policies have extended this unevenness.

Free trade and transnational labour solidarity

As a result of this unevenness, different national trade unions are in different positions within global capitalism. Unsurprisingly, although workers from around the world are exploited in capitalist social relations of production, this does not automatically imply that it will be in their immediate and obvious interest to join forces. As indicated above in the example of the WTO Doha negotiations in 2008, this expanded free trade agenda has led to tensions within the global labour movement. On the one hand, trade unions in the North, especially in manufacturing, have supported FTAs. They hope that new export markets for products in their sectors will preserve jobs. On the other hand, trade unions in the South oppose these FTAs since they often imply de-industrialisation and the related loss of jobs for them. As a result, transnational solidarity is difficult to achieve.

And yet, the fact that different national labour movements are located in different positions in the global economy does not imply that transnational solidarity is impossible. The experience of trade unions in the Americas is illustrative in this respect. When the North American Free Trade Agreement (NAFTA) came into force on 1 January 1994, there was no common trade union position. While the Canadian Labour Congress had opposed it, the main Mexican trade union confederation supported the agreement. US trade unions presented a mixed picture. As a result of experiences with NAFTA, however, a common position has emerged over time. This new position does not only include a rejection of neoliberal FTAs such as the defeated Free Trade Area of the Americas (FTAA) initiative. It also 'seeks to design a model of integration that is an alternative to free trade, not only because it proposes alternative trade rules, but because it aims at moving away from neoliberalism by giving a new centrality to the State, and to a new democratic and participatory process' (Ciccaglione, 2009: 30).

The related strategies include both cross-border cooperation with trade unions as well as alliances with other social movements. Thus, they, provide the basis for a common consciousness at the transnational level. As a result of concrete struggles against free trade initiatives in the Americas, labour has moved towards transnational solidarity. Such forms of transnational solidarity may in turn provide the basis for developing new ways of trade organisation between countries. The Bolivarian Alliance for the Americas (ALBA), for example, is already one practical example in this respect. When it began in 2004, it was a treaty between Venezuela and Cuba with the former providing petroleum to the latter at very favourable prices in exchange for doctors and teachers from Cuba, working in some of Venezuela's poorest states. Direct negotiations between the two countries had replaced a reliance on prices set by the market.

Global North and global South, core and periphery are not fixed categories, but are constituted and re-constituted by concrete social relations. In response to the global economic crisis, working relations are increasingly becoming informal in industrialised countries too. There is also an increase in low-wage service sector jobs. In other words, the traditional global South is also emerging in the global North – the periphery in the core – and clear boundaries are disappearing. The realisation by workers in the North that further free trade also requires further deregulation and liberalisation in the North and is, thus, harmful to them too may provide the basis for more active transnational solidarity. Samir Amin, the keynote speaker at a workshop on 'Trade unions, free trade and the problem of transnational solidarity', held at Nottingham University in December 2011, demanded 'audacity, more audacity, always audacity' in the search for alternatives, including a move towards delinking from today's neoliberal globalisation. This would allow nations with advanced radical social and political struggles to move towards a process of socialisation of the management of their economy. Relations of transnational solidarity between labour movements in the South and North are possible if such calls for audacity are heard and delinking is put into practice.

References

Bieler, A. (2013) 'The EU, Global Europe and processes of uneven and combined development: the problem of transnational labour solidarity', *Review of International Studies*, Vol. 39, No. 1.

Bieler, A., Ciccaglione, B., Hilary, J., and Lindberg, I. (eds) (2014) *Free Trade and Transnational Labour* (London: Routledge).

Ciccaglione, B. (2009) *Free Trade and Trade Unions of the Americas: Strategies, practices, Struggles, Achievements* (Vienna: Chamber of Labour). Available from http://media.arbeiterkammer.at/wien/PDF/studien/FreeTradeandTrade Unions.pdf.

Hilary, J. (2014) *The Transatlantic Trade and Investment Partnership (TTIP): A charter for Deregulation, an Attack on Jobs, an End to Democracy* (Brussels: Rosa-Luxemburg Foundation).

Mandel, E. (1975) *Late Capitalism* (London: New Left Books).

War on Want (2009) *Trading Away Our Jobs: How Free Trade Threatens Employment Around the World* (London: War on Want). Available from www.waronwant.org.

28

Modelling a Global Union Strategy: The Arena of Global Production Networks, Global Framework Agreements and Trade Union Networks

Michael Fichter

For the past decades of economic globalisation, unions around the world have been on the defensive; their role as voices of the political and economic interests of working people has been marginalised. In a climate of outsourcing, offshoring, flexibilisation and casualisation of work, the loss of union power and the deregulation of labour markets has flourished and opened the way for increasing precariousness and agency work. Permanent jobs are being replaced by the 'triangular trap', locking workers into employment relationships in which they are officially employed by an agency or contractor, but actually working for another company (IndustriALL, 2012).

While continuing to fight to protect their hard-won regulatory instruments within their national domains, trade unions have also begun to look for transnational approaches to combat unfettered international competition that is fed by a race to the bottom over labour costs. The challenge is in developing a strategy that will serve as a political and organisational answer to the dilemma they face – namely, how to bring the power of unions, as locally or nationally organised entities, to bear on the transnational regulation gap in labour relations.

Global Framework Agreements: a tool of union power

I would argue that the most important tool unions have devised to embark on this task is the Global Framework Agreement (GFA). In contrast to the unilateral and voluntary character of Corporate Social Responsibility (CSR) measures, GFAs are bilateral, negotiated and signed as a policy document between transnational corporations (TNCs) and Global Union Federations (GUFs). Based primarily on the International Labour Organisation's (ILO) Core Labour Standards and other ILO Conventions, they lay a foundation for conducting labour relations in a delineated space or arena, that is, throughout the operations of a TNC and its global network of suppliers, sub-contractors, and other business partners. GFAs also include mechanisms for monitoring as well as procedures for internal conflict resolution.

During the 1970s, efforts at bringing the collective voice of labour into the TNC power equation through world company councils failed; they were ignored by the TNCs they were supposed to influence. Attempts at regulating TNCs through lobbying at international institutions have been largely ineffective as the unsuccessful bid to anchor a 'social clause' in the WTO in the 1990s demonstrated. Instead, global unions turned to meeting TNCs head on, responding to the spread of corporate codes of conduct and unilateral CSR policies with GFAs. And since 2000 – more than a decade after the first GFA was signed – the number has grown exponentially; today there are more than 100 signed agreements, of which over 90 are currently active.

Empirical research confirms implementation deficits

In a three-year multinational research project funded by the union-supported Hans Boeckler Foundation in Germany, we analysed all 73 GFAs signed before 2011 and took a sample of 16 of them for case studies of their implementation. All 16 agreements were signed with corporations headquartered in the European Union (EU) and with subsidiaries in four countries from four different continents with different national systems of labour relations and different positions in the global division of labour: Brazil, India, Turkey and the USA.

GFAs are a milestone initiative. But as our field research shows, and as many critics – including unionists – have pointed out, there are still miles to go. In all four countries we found a widespread lack of implementation. This can be explained by a combination of factors. While implementation is left up to local actors, these representatives of labour and management are rarely directly involved in the negotiation of GFAs (Fichter et al., 2012; Arruda, et al., 2012). Thus, they lack a sense of 'ownership'.

Secondly, the existence of GFAs was largely unknown among managers in TNC subsidiaries and in the local trade unions. Often, the agreement had not been disseminated to the subsidiaries, or if it had been, its significance as a joint labour-management policy regulation, applicable throughout the corporation, had not been adequately conveyed to the local actors. When unions did know about the GFA, they generally had no understanding as to how they could use the agreement to gain recognition and to support a bargaining agenda.

For its part, management preferred to disregard the joint labour-management character of the agreements. Instead, the provisions of many agreements can be found unilaterally embedded in the company's CSR agenda with no reference to them having been negotiated with the unions. Finally, we found that most local unions, if active at all internationally, were only tentatively or very weakly linked to unions in other countries or to the GUFs.

Building a union strategy around Global Framework Agreements

However, at the same time, we found evidence of GFAs being successfully used in certain cases (see Helfen, 2011). They differ from the cases with poor or no implementation because unions used the GFA strategically as a policy instrument, prioritised its implementation, and mobilised the necessary resources. Unfortunately, this kind of approach is more the exception than the rule. Indeed, some emphasise that it is imperative for the GUFs together with their affiliates to begin moving beyond the current stop-gap, case-by-case crisis management approach to a more pro-active strategic policy.

By strategy, I mean unions need to work toward improving the quality of GFA content. Many agreements in existence today are vague and easily open to widely differing interpretation. Verbatim incorporation of the ILO Core Labour Standards is absolutely basic. Additional ILO Conventions such as workplace representation or health and safety add significantly to the quality. Rarely used up to now but equally essential are guarantees of management neutrality toward union organising drives and regulated access to the workplace for unions. Furthermore, the relationship between global norms and national laws needs to be more explicit: The most stringent standard must prevail.

Secondly, GFAs need to define clearly the arena of their applicability as extending coverage beyond the immediate boundaries of the TNC to cover all its global value network. Union policy that stops at the organisational boundary of a TNC is too limited; it needs to include the whole system of suppliers, sub-contractors, service and sales units and – increasingly – manpower (agency) services. Only then is there a possibility of leveraging union strength and linking local institutional settings of labour relations.

As for the actors involved in the GFA process, in the past, negotiations have been conducted by GUFs, by home country unions and sometimes by company works councils – and not always in harmony with each other. Handing over negotiations to works councils is highly problematic in regard to the recognition and implementation of a global agreement between autonomous actors. Instead, I argue that mutual recognition means management negotiates with the GUF, and that there is a plan for involvement of GUF affiliates and local management, the ones responsible for implementation. The procedures anchored in the agreement need to define implementation as a joint task, starting with joint information and communication, extending to joint training programmes and rounding out the process using joint reviews and initiating the implementation of organisational practices that reflect the principles of the agreement (Sydow et al., 2014).

Beyond the GFA: transnational union networking

Having a GFA is an important step, but without implementation it remains powerless. To challenge the power of transnational corporations using GFAs, unions need to build transnational union networks as a complementary step in a global union strategy. To be effective, such networks must have clearly defined goals, including initiating, negotiating and implementing the GFA, organising 'ownership' of the agreement throughout the union network, raising the leverage potential of local/national affiliates, using the GFA as a space to organise, and building and strengthening cross-border cooperation and solidarity.

And they must be organised along clear principles of governance. That requires having defined leadership structures constructed around the GUF or a key affiliate, agreed priorities and assigned division of responsibilities, and a full commitment of resources.

GFAs are not a strategy in themselves. Nor does their signing per se create new, transnational arenas of labour relations. Without active, focused and coordinated union input, they remain dormant. Transnational union networks can make them into a tool for developing a strategy of union voice in TNCs and among their far-flung suppliers, sub-contractors and other business partners. In the past, the tendency was to regard implementation of a GFA as a management prerogative. But management has basically reneged in actively meeting this task. And for GUFs or home country unions to base their GFA policies on such expectations makes it very difficult to get local unions at the subsidiary and supplier level involved. GFAs are a joint labour-management statement and as such need to be jointly implemented. Ownership comes through common strategy. Building participation through transnational union networks during negotiations is a precondition for strengthening implementation.

GFAs have opened the way for unions to engage TNCs on a global level. And the realisation has spread that such agreements can be successfully used to organise unions and gain recognition. Building union cooperation and strength around GFAs is potentially a means of concentrating union resources in a defined arena as a basis for moving toward a comprehensive transnational political strategy for global labour relations.

References

Arruda, L. et al. (2012) *'International Framework Agreements: A Powerful Tool for Ensuring Core Labor Standards in a Globalized World? Insights from Brazil* (Friedrich-Ebert-Foundation). Available from http://library.fes.de.

Fichter, M., Sydow, J., Helfen, M., Arruda, L., Agtas, Ö., Gartenberg, I., Mccallum, J. and Stevis, D. (2012) *Globalising Labour Relations: On Track with Framework Agreements?* (Berlin: Friedrich-Ebert-Foundation). Available from http://library.fes.de.

Helfen, M. (2011) 'Going local with global policies: Implementing international framework agreements in Brazil and the United States', in K. Papadakis (ed.) *Shaping Global Industrial Relation: The Impact of International Framework Agreements* (Houndsmills: Palgrave Macmillan).

IndustriALL (2012) *The Triangular Trap: Unions Take Action Against Agency Labour* (Geneva: IndustriALL). Available from www.industriall-union.org.

Sydow, J., Fichter, M., Helfen, M., Sayim, K.Z. and Stevis, D. (2014) 'Implementation of Global Framework Agreements: Towards a Multi-organizational Practice Perspective', *Transfer*, Vol. 20, No. 4.

29

Trade Unions, Globalisation and Internationalism

Ronaldo Munck

This chapter reports on recent research around the relationship between trade unions and internationalisation in the context of globalisation. It argues for a more open, less pessimistic view than the dominant one. This view builds on the experiences of the 1970s and is cognisant of the depth of the current crisis.

Transnationalism

Unions and the workers they represent have always been part of a transnational system of labour relations. Capital has always been mobile and the capital/wage-labour relation has never been hermetically contained within national boundaries. However, until quite recently, the dominant system of industrial relations had been confined, almost exclusively, within a national frame. In the 1970s, a 'new' international division of labour emerged as the ex-colonial countries began to industrialise and the multinational corporations became central players in the neo-colonial global system. This period saw a major flourishing of transnational labour activity and the hope, soon dashed, that union internationalism could act as a 'countervailing power' to that of the multinationals.

Later, in the 1990s, the era of globalisation began, characterised by the hegemony of neoliberal economics, the victory of the West in the Cold War and the rise of international institutions such as the World Trade Organisation. The international union movement was unified during this phase and clearly recognised the major challenges posed by globalisation to a 'business as usual' approach. Today, with the unravelling of the neoliberal consensus and its whole global development model in 2008, a new period of crisis and uncertainty opens up (Munck, 2010a).

Labour internationalism will not emerge spontaneously with that of capital as though capital's global reach automatically generates labour internationalism. Internationalism should rather be seen as a political project that needs to be constructed. Nor is it a timeless political project reaching back seamlessly to the formation of the First International in 1864. Nor does labour internationalism trump all other forms of union activity at the local, national and regional levels.

Transitional 1970s

From a present-day perspective, the 1970s and 1980s could probably be viewed as a transitional period. Capitalism at a global level began to hit structural contradictions which would finally unravel in the crisis of 2008–09. However, as the class struggle intensified, capitalism prepared for the great leap forward under neoliberal globalisation. Workers and their unions in the North began an incipient process of transnational organisation. While not resulting in the transnational collective bargaining many hoped for, it did begin to break down its nation-statist attitudes. The global South was beginning to play a more important role with many new labour initiatives being pioneered in this world zone.

While we might question the dualism of counter-posing 'objective' conditions and subjective responses by labour to them, this phase of global history set the terrain for a hugely expanded global labour force and for greater interactions between its national and sectoral fractions. It also laid the basis for capital to take a great leap forward to overcome its inherent contradictions and to strengthen its position in relation to an increasingly uncooperative Western working class and a South in open revolt.

There are major sectoral differentiations in terms of the modalities and effectiveness of transnational union activity. The global competition at the heart of neoliberal globalisation severely weakened the organising capacity of unions. So, unions have responded to offshoring, for example, through the establishment of international union links. In some sectors such as transportation there was a long history of international solidarity to build on. Thus in the shipping sector the International Transport Workers' Federation (ITF) now acts effectively on behalf of its members across the globe setting wages and effectively campaigning against the 'flags of convenience'. In the air transport sector representation at a transnational level is not so strong; however, unions have contested the restructuring/flexibility agenda of the employers. In the motor industry, a key locus in the 1980s attempts to create cross-plant union networks, there was a flourishing of company level World Employee Committees which allowed workers to share information between themselves and with management across borders.

However uneven and differentiated the process of internationalisation has been since 2000, unionists have increasingly challenged unfettered capitalist control over the labour market. We can see that in particular branches of industry or areas of the world (such as Latin America) as well as a broader international labour revival since 2000 with a plethora of initiatives by international unions at both the official and grassroots levels.

Resurgence post-2000

In the early 2000s international labour activity found considerable resonance and reached levels only dreamt of in the 1970s. Transnational communication and networking had become easier and many of the political obstacles had been overcome. Now even the seemingly most localised struggle needs to adopt a global optic. Indeed, we could argue that there is a new local-global terrain which does not necessarily 'pass through' its national level. Local struggles may turn to transnational repertoires of actions directly. We can envisage a more complex unionism as a multi-level response to globalisation which has impacted on workers at local, national and regional levels as well as at the transnational level.

It is highly debatable whether the international union movement has entirely overcome the structural and political impediments to full international labour solidarity. With the International Secretariats quite removed from the workplace, their solidarity campaigns may appear remote to shop floor activists. With most national unions still committed to an outdated concept of 'partnership', international solidarity is reduced to a ritual. A new perspective, or rather a revival of the 1970s one, would recognise the social role of labour and the unions which have been confined to their economic and political roles for too long. The challenge is to take this perspective, which played a role in combating authoritarian regimes in the South by constructing a community unionism, and 'scale it up' globally (Munck, 2010b).

Retrospective

In retrospect, globalisation probably opened as many doors for labour as it closed. Neoliberalism as a dominant capital accumulation strategy represented a class offensive against workers and their representative organisations. Labour recovered a considerable amount of its organisational capacity during this phase. By the end of this period the inherent contradictions of capitalism had re-emerged with a vengeance with the great bubble of financial speculation that drove its final phase. The capitalist crisis began to unravel in 2007 but it reached a critical point in September 2008 as a number of major 'name' banks failed. There was simply no trust left in the basic financial intermediation mechanism which underpins the capitalist system. As capitalism's 'credit crunch' turned into a global recession in 2008 the union movement was at first taken aback, as were many sectors in society. The spectre of the 1930s recession was uppermost in many people's minds. By early 2009 there was at least a clearer analysis and a credible alternative being presented by the global unions, even if this was not translated into practice due to the lack of social power to impose it. Their statement to the London G20 Summit in April 2009 accepted that there was no return to 'business as usual' and went on to argue that: 'The crisis must mark the end of an ideology of unfettered financial markets, where self-regulation has been exposed as a fraud and greed has overridden rational judgment to the detriment of the real economy' (Global Unions London Declaration, 2009). Nothing less than a redrawing of the governance of the global economy to foreground social (and environmental) issues would suffice. However, the means proposed to implement this alternative programme – a revival of the post-war tripartite structures involving government, capital and labour – seemed somewhat of an anachronism given its inherent limitations even in the once affluent North where this corporatist model had some purchase.

Back to the future?

If labour internationalism first became a significant factor in the pre-national phase, what are its prospects today in what we might call a 'post-national' phase of global history? Looking towards the future of unions we might posit a 'back to the future' type of strategy with internationalism as its core philosophy. The era of globalisation has created a novel and complex terrain for labour internationalism where local, regional and global levels interact and where community, consumption and production levels are all present. We can no longer afford to ignore the complex interplay of the spatial dimension of labour activity, not least when dealing with the international, once seen as a separate domain from the national or local, higher or lower in terms of hierarchy according to one's political stance.

The future of labour internationalism does not hinge around whether as labour analysts we are optimists or pessimists. What is important is to recognise the major shifts that have occurred over the past 20 years as labour has rebuilt at least some of its structures that had been decimated by neoliberalism. If labour is now catching up with capital's long campaign of internationalisation (known as globalisation) then it may now be the turn of labour to become globalised (Munck, 2010c).

References

Global Unions London Declaration (2009) 'Statement to the London G20 Summit'. Available from www.ituc-csi.org.

Munck, R. (2010a) 'Globalization, Crisis and Social Transformation: A View from the South', *Globalizations*, Vol. 7, No. 1–2.

Munck, R. (2010b) 'Globalization, Migration and Decent Work: Global Issues and Perspectives', *Labour, Capital and Society / Travail, Capital et Société*, Vol. 43, No. 1.

Munck, R. (2010c) 'Globalization and the Labour Movement: Challenges and Responses', *Global Labour Journal*, Vol. 1, No. 2.

30

Chinese Construction Companies in Africa: A Challenge for Trade Unions

Eddie Cottle

The Chinese-built African Union (AU) headquarters, in Addis Ababa, are a bold symbol of China's rapidly changing role in Africa. China-African relations run as far deep as China being the biggest supporter of Africa's anti-colonial struggle and the first to assist reconstruction efforts for the newly formed African States. The most famous example is the 1,800km Tanzania–Zambia Railway (Tazara) that was built in the 1970s by some 50,000 Chinese engineers and workers, during which 64 of these workers died. China had provided a US$400 million interest-free loan to build the railway, at a time when it was poorer than most African countries (Monson, 2009). After two decades of negative growth for most sub-Saharan countries, the end of apartheid in South Africa and the 1996 visit of Chinese President Jiang Zemin to Africa set a new course in Chino–African relations (Johnston and Yuan, 2014).

Chinese investment boosts African economic growth and infrastructure

China's rapidly growing economy has made it crucial to secure energy resources for its development in the future. In this regard, Africa's importance to China's overseas investment agenda is significant. In July 2012, President Hu Jintao pledged $20 billion in credit for Africa for lucrative investment and infrastructure – critical and to the annoyance of the West is China's no-strings attached loans. Two years before that, in 2010, China and Ghana signed an agreement for a 20-year loan of $13.1 billion with an interest payment of only 2 per cent. There is increasing fear over this arrangement that it might lead African countries to opt-out of International Monetary Fund and World Bank loans and other forms of credit dependence on Europe and the US (Beattie & Callen, 2006).

Over 2,000 Chinese state-owned companies (SOEs) have now established businesses in Africa. In 2013 the World Bank claimed that 55 per cent of all African investment projects were now driven by private enterprises. Two-way trade between China and Africa reached $166 billion in 2011 and $198 billion by 2012. Compared to the approximate $2 billion in 1999 this is a huge jump, making China the largest individual trading partner in Africa. The largest single investment by China in Africa was however in the financial sector, when in 2008 China's Industrial and Commercial Bank (ICBC) acquired a 20 per cent stake of South Africa's Standard Bank. (Lawrence, 2014). By late 2013 various Chinese state banks have announced that they will make a combined investment of some $1 trillion over twelve years (Rotberg, 2013). Trade with China, including massive investment, has directly contributed to the significant increase in average African economic growth of 5.3 per cent in the period 2000–10, 2 percentage points above the world average (UNCTAD, 2014).

Chinese state-owned and private companies are making strategic inroads into the construction and infrastructure sectors in many African economies. The head of Vinci, the world's largest concessions and construction company, indicated that Chinese firms often submit bids three-quarters lower than Western firms. Furthermore, Chinese engineers are paid approximately US$130 per month, one-sixth of what European construction firms pay Angolan engineers (Guliwe, 2009). Chinese companies now dominate the African construction sector, with a market share larger than those of France, Italy and the US combined. The share of Chinese enterprises in the African market rose significantly from 26.9 per cent in 2007 to 42.4 per cent in 2008 and down to 36.6 per cent in 2009 (Liu and Stocken, 2012).

Rail infrastructure in Angola, one of China's top oil suppliers, is rapidly expanding as part of an infrastructure-for-oil trade agreement between the two countries. Kenya recently signed a $5 billion deal with China to construct a 952km rail link from the city port of Mombasa to Malaba, a town near its border with Uganda. This is expected to be extended to Rwanda, Uganda and Tanzania by 2018.

In September 2012, the China Railway Construction Corp (CRC) signed a $1.5 billion contract to rehabilitate a railway system in Nigeria. The CRC has ongoing projects in Djibouti, Ethiopia and Nigeria worth about $1.5 billion in total.

China South Locomotive and Rolling Stock Corporation, a major train manufacturer in China, is bringing in $400 million-worth of locomotives to South Africa. And China's Export–Import Bank is financing the Mombasa–Nairobi railroad line with $4 billion, while the Addis Ababa–Djibouti line is being rehabilitated at a cost of $3 billion. In August 2014, China Railway 20 Bureau Group Corporation (CR20) completed the $1.83 billion reconstruction of the Benguela railway that connects Angola, Zambia and southeastern Democratic Republic of the Congo (Barber, 2014).

African trade unions challenge Chinese companies

The issue of poor labour standards has been one of the most controversial aspects of Chinese investments – pitting trade unions against Chinese companies and government officials. Strikes have increased in various African states, the most recent of which was against the China Harbour Engineering Company (CHEC) at Namport, Namibia; it was precipitated by the suspension of 72 workers who accused the company of unfair labour practices, favouritism, abuse and intimidation (New Era, 2013).

Research by the Building and Wood Workers' International union federation (BWI) found that there was strong non-compliance with payment of the minimum wage rates in Namibia (Cottle, 2012). Only *half* the required legal rate was paid, whereas in both Tanzania and Zambia there was compliance; in Tanzania, Chinese companies even paid a bit more than the minimum rate. The report found that labour standards in Tanzania and Namibia have improved marginally since 2005, when the companies were found to be flouting most basic conditions of employment and health and safety standards. In Zambia the research found that the state owned construction companies, China Geo-Engineering and China Civil

Engineering Construction Corporation, generally complied with labour legislation and health and safety but that the private construction company Yangst Jiang was rampantly flouting labour legislation. In all the countries under this study the vast majority of workers employed on worksites were nationals employed largely as casual labour in unskilled and semi-skilled positions. While the trade unions have been too weak to impose compliance with labour law, it appears that they are beginning to become more effective in taking up the workplace challenges, such as improving wages. Despite the odds, African trade unions affiliated to BWI have signed a landmark collective bargaining agreement and are actively recruiting workers on Chinese SOE's worksites.

A good part of these successes has to do with the fact that BWI has, since 2007, ensured consistent dialogue with its affiliates at its African regional meetings where various strategies were deliberated and planned. Specific projects (partly financed by BWI) and campaigns were formulated to defend workers' rights and living standards. By early 2013, the Ghana Construction and Building Materials Workers Union (CBMWU) had signed eight collective agreements with different Chinese companies. The collective contract includes recognition of trade unions, union security clauses, individual and collective rights, procedural processes for addressing conflicts over interests and rights, monetary and non-monetary provisions, paid vacation leaves and exit packages. Similarly, the Kenya Building, Construction, Timber and Furniture Industries Employees Union have been able to sign four collective agreements with China Road and Bridge Corporation, China Sinohydro Cooperation, China Overseas Corporation, and China Jiangsu International.

In 2012, the Uganda construction union (UBCCECAWU) recruited more than 200 female members and over 1,600 male members in the above mentioned companies. The union has also recruited workers from some of the notoriously difficult Chinese employers, including China Sinohydro Construction Corporation (Ntugamo project) and China Chonguing International Construction Corporation (CICO).

BWI research in Tanzania found that Chinese companies were violating the Freedom of Association of the Employment and Labour Relations Act of Tanzania. In Namibia and Zambia, the trade unions had access to company sites and were organising and recruiting members freely, including having recognition agreements and concluding collective agreements. Thus,

African construction trade unions have taken the global lead in the labour movement in organising and bargaining with Chinese construction firms.

China's economic involvement on the continent has been accompanied with speculation that its role has shifted from that of a supporter of Africa's liberation to one as a neo-colonial power, competing with the West for influence in a new 'Scramble for Africa'. However, other scholars have argued that the Asian power is largely following the same grand strategy it pursued from 1954 until the present: that of not interfering with conditionalities in the domestic policies of African states. Furthermore, African countries have welcomed China's non-interference strategy which has been viewed as a refreshing departure from the prescriptive policy of the West which forced African leaders into the straitjacket of structural adjustment programmes (Lawrence, 2014).

Extending the struggle to FOCAC

At the Forum on China–Africa Cooperation (FOCAC) V, in 2012, African leaders openly tabled the contentious issues in the relationship with China which were once avoided at previous FOCAC meetings. China responded in favour of infrastructure development in line with Africa's own regional integration projects as well as promoting greater product beneficiation in the resource sector (Centre for Chinese Studies, 2014). Finally, South Africa's role as host of the upcoming FOCAC in 2015 places it in a unique position to influence the tenor and trajectory of this longstanding collaborative initiative. This context provides a key opportunity for ITUC-Africa, BWI and South Africa's trade union federations to launch a campaign to place labour firmly on the agenda of the forthcoming FOCAC VI meeting and in so doing would add a completely new dimension to Chinese–African relations.

References

Barber, D. (2014) 'Will Africa's Transportation Infrastructure Development Be Sustainable?'. Available from www.afkinsider.com.

Beattie, A., and Callan, E. (2006) 'China loans create new wave of African Debt', *FT.com*. Available from www.ft.com.

Centre for Chinese Studies. (2014) 'Putting the CAP in FOCAC: How African countries can get on the FOCAC train for South Africa', 2015 China–Africa Forum. Available from www.ccs.org.za.

Cottle, E. (2012) 'Case studies on Chinese companies' labour practices in the African construction sector', Building and Wood Workers' International (unpublished).

Guliwe, T. (2009) 'An introduction to Chinese–African relations', in Baah, A.Y. and Jauch, H. (eds), *Chinese Investments in Africa: A Labour Perspective* (Johannesburg: African Labour Research Network).

Johnston, L. and Yuan, C. (2014) 'China's Africa Trade and Investment Policies: Review of a "Noodle Bowl"', Centre for Chinese Studies, *The China Monitor*, No. 4.

Lawrence, O.A. (2014) 'From non-interference to preponderance: China's future grand strategy in Africa', *The China Monitor*, No. 2. Available from www.ccs.org.za.

Liu, B. and Stocken, R. (2012) 'Africa: Why Chinese Companies Are Successful in Africa', *All Africa*. Available from http://allafrica.com.

Monson, J. (2009) *Africa's Freedom Railway: How a Chinese Development Project Changed Lives and Livelihoods in Tanzania* (Bloomington: Indiana University Press).

New Era (2013) 'Namibia: Strike Disrupts Port Construction'. Available from http://allafrica.com.

Rotberg, R. (2013) 'China's $1 Trillion for Africa'. Available from www.chinausfocus.com.

UNCTAD (2014) *Economic Development in Africa: Catalysing Investment for Transformative Growth in Africa* (Geneva: United Nations).

Notes on Contributors

Giorgos Argitis is Professor of Economics, University of Athens and Research Director of the Labour Institute-Greek General Confederation of Labour, email: gargeitis@econ.uoa.gr.

Dennis Arnold is Assistant Professor at the University of Amsterdam, Department of Human Geography, Planning and International Development. Drawing on research in Cambodia, Myanmar, Thailand and Vietnam, Dennis' work focuses on labour and migration; global production network analysis; and borders of continental Southeast Asia. His papers are available at: http://uva.academia.edu/DennisArnold.

Sam Ashman is an Associate Professor at the University of Johannesburg.

Andreas Bieler is Professor of Political Economy at Nottingham University, UK and Fellow of the Centre for the Study of Social and Global Justice (CSSGJ). For further details, see his personal website (http://andreasbieler. net/) or his blog Trade Unions and Global Restructuring (http:// andreasbieler.blogspot.co.uk/).

Ruth Castel-Branco is a Mozambican researcher, writer and labour activist. Her current area of focus is on labour process, social protection and worker rights.

Anis Chowdhury is the Director of the Statistics Division at the Economic and Social Commission for Asia and the Pacific (UN-ESCAP), Bangkok.

Cédric Durand is an Associate Professor of Economics at the University of Paris 13 (CEPN – CNRS) and a member of the 'Économistes atterrés' collective. His current research focuses on the relationship between financialisation and globalisation and the political economy of the crisis in Europe.

João Antônio Felício is Secretary for International Relations of the Brazilian Central Única dos Trabalhadores (CUT) and President of the International Trade Union Confederation (ITUC). João has been working as a teacher in the public education system of the state of São Paulo since 1973. His political activism and trade union engagement started in 1977 when he participated in the strikes against the military dictatorship in Brazil.

Lisa Carstensen is a doctoral fellow at the Global Social Policies and Governance (GSPG) Programme at the University of Kassel. Her research analyses modern slave labour in global production networks in Brazil from a postcolonial point of view.

Karl Cloete is Deputy General Secretary of NUMSA, the National Union of Metalworkers of South Africa.

Eddie Cottle is the former policy and campaign coordinator of BWI, Africa & Middle East Region and is currently employed at the Labour Research Service, Cape Town, South Africa.

Michael Fichter is a political scientist and on the teaching staff of the Global Labour University in Germany. He has done extensive research on global labour relations, including a recently completed research project on Global Framework Agreements. Website: www.polsoz.fu-berlin.de/polwiss/ifa_projekt.

Tandiwe Gross works as a programme coordinator for the Global Labour University and as a labour researcher and activist in various trade unions and NGO networks. Her research is focused on human rights, due diligence in global supply chains, corporate accountability and informal and precarious employment relationships.

Christoph Hermann is a senior researcher at the Working Life Research Centre, Vienna, and a lecturer at the University of Vienna (Austria).

Hansjörg Herr is Professor for Supranational Integration at the Berlin School of Economics and Law and at his university the co-ordinator for the MA Labour Policies and Globalisation of the Global Labour University.

Frank Hoffer is senior research officer at the Bureau for Workers' Activities of the ILO.

Carlo D'Ippoliti is Assistant Professor of Economics at Sapienza University of Rome, and assistant editor of *PSL Quarterly Review* (www.pslquarterlyreview.info) and *Moneta e Credito* (www.monetaecredito.info).

He is the author of *Economics and Diversity* (Routledge, 2011) and *Crisi: (come) ne usciamo?* (L'asino d'oro, 2012).

Carol Jess is an MA graduate in International Labour and Trade Union Studies at Ruskin College, Oxford, UK. She was a trade union activist in the UK, before moving to New Zealand where she is researching the trade union movement's strategies for renewal as a PhD thesis, with the Centre for Labour, Employment and Work at Victoria University of Wellington. She is also active in New Zealand politics and combines this with teaching various aspects of industrial and employment relations.

Peter Knorringa is Professor of Private Sector & Development at the International Institute of Social Studies (ISS) of Erasmus University Rotterdam in The Hague, the Netherlands. His research focuses on how business co-shapes conditions for labour and sustainability.

Dany Lang is an Associate Professor of Economics at the University of Paris 13 (CEPN – CNRS) and a member of the 'Économistes atterrés' collective. His research is on post-Keynesian economics, including growth, income distribution, unemployment issues and path-dependency.

Frederic Sterling Lee was a Professor of Economics at the University of Missouri-Kansas City. He taught at De Montfort University in the UK in the 1990s. Professor Lee passed away in 2014 after a long battle against cancer.

Janine Leschke is Associate Professor at the Department of Business and Politics (DBP) at Copenhagen Business School. Her research interests are related to labour market and welfare state analysis in a European comparative perspective.

Siobhán McGrath is a Lecturer in Human Geography at Durham University. Her research interests include labour relations, Global Production Networks (GPNs) and Brazil as a rising power.

Jeroen Merk is a David Davies of Llandinam Fellow at the London School of Economics, UK, where he works on the project 'Re-inventing corporate accountability after the Rana Plaza collapse'.

Phoebe V. Moore is a Senior Lecturer in International Relations at the University of Middlesex, London. She lectures and writes about labour struggles, industrial relations and the impact of technology on everyday lives.

Ronaldo Munck is Head of Civic and Global Engagement at Dublin City University in Ireland (www.dcu.ie/community). He writes about labour and social transformation as well as Latin America.

Mbuso Nkosi is the son of Mzikayifani Brian Dongo and Didi Thokozane Nkosi. He is a PhD candidate (Development Studies) at the University of Witwatersrand. He serves as the co-editor of the Global Labour Column.

Tony Norfield is currently researching for a PhD on 'British imperialism and finance' at the School of Oriental and African Studies in London. His interests are centred on using Marxist theory to understand the contemporary imperialist world economy. Prior to this he had worked for nearly 20 years in bank dealing rooms analysing financial markets and had been Global Head of FX Strategy for a major European bank. He writes a blog on the 'Economics of Imperialism'. His blog can be found at http://economicsofimperialism.blogspot.com/.

Özlem Onaran is a Professor of Workforce and Economic Development Policy at the University of Greenwich, UK.

Thomas Palley is Senior Economic Adviser to the American Federation of Labor and Congress of Industrial Organizations (AFL–CIO) and an Associate of the Economic Growth Program of the New America Foundation in Washington. D.C. His most recent book is *From Financial Crisis to Stagnation: The Destruction of Shared Prosperity and the Role of Economics* (Cambridge: Cambridge University Press, 2012). His op-eds are posted on his website www.thomaspalley.com.

Vasco Pedrina is a former Co-President of Unia and USS (Swiss Trade Union Confederation), former Vice-President of BWI (Building and Wood Workers' International) and a board-member of the Global Labour Institute.

Nicolas Pons-Vignon is a Senior Researcher in the School of Economic and Business Science at the University of the Witwatersrand.

Karin Astrid Siegmann is a Senior Lecturer in Labour and Gender Economics at the International Institute of Social Studies (ISS) of Erasmus

University Rotterdam in The Hague, the Netherlands. Her research is concerned with gendered labour dimensions in global production networks, international migration and financial crises.

Paul Stewart teaches at the University of the Witwatersrand, South Africa. He lived in the mineworkers' compounds and went underground daily to do research for his PhD thesis entitled: 'Labour time on the South African gold mines: 1886–2006'. Together with Dhiraj Nite, he edited a book entitled *Mining Faces: An Oral History of Work in Gold and Coal Mines in South Africa: 1951–2011* (Johannesburg: Fanele/Jacana).

Ilan Strauss is an economics PhD student at the New School, New York City. He holds an MSc in Development Economics from SOAS (University of London). He has worked as a consultant for the United Nations Economic Commission for Africa (UNECA), African Development Bank (AfDB), and Trade and Industrial Policies (TIPS). He currently works as a consultant for UNCTAD on FDI.

Jomo Kwame Sundaram is Coordinator for Economic and Social Development at the Food and Agricultural Organisation (FAO), Rome.

Salimah Valiani is Associate Researcher at the Centre for Learning, Social Economy and Work, University of Toronto, and author of *Rethinking Unequal Exchange: The Global Integration of Nursing Labour Markets* (Toronto: University of Toronto Press, 2012).

Andrew Watt is Deputy Head of the Macroeconomic Policy Institute (IMK), part of the Hans-Böckler Foundation. His main fields are European economic and employment policy. Regular blogs and columns appear at: www.social-europe.eu/author/andrew-watt/.

Roland Zullo is an Associate Research Scientist at the Institute for Research on Labor, Employment and the Economy at the University of Michigan. Zullo researches union strategy, privatisation, outsourcing, political mobilisation, collective bargaining, and critical pedagogy.

Index

Compiled by Sue Carlton